Henry H Vowles

For Ever and Ever

A Popular Story in Hebrew, Greek and English

Henry H Vowles

For Ever and Ever
A Popular Story in Hebrew, Greek and English

ISBN/EAN: 9783744664257

Printed in Europe, USA, Canada, Australia, Japan

Cover: Foto ©Lupo / pixelio.de

More available books at **www.hansebooks.com**

"FOR EVER AND EVER"

A Popular Study

IN

HEBREW, GREEK, AND ENGLISH WORDS

BY

HENRY H. VOWLES

Our poets make poems out of words; but every word, if carefully examined, will turn out to be itself a petrified poem.—PROFESSOR MAX MÜLLER.

LONDON
SWAN SONNENSCHEIN & CO., LIM.
PATERNOSTER SQUARE
1898

PREFACE

THIS book, which gives an account of a supposed discovery in Biblical philology, is the outcome of an endeavour to ascertain the exact sense of words, and of a conviction that prophets and apostles were not likely to speak of unprovable things.

The writing of it has been influenced by an opinion that all intelligent persons, and not scholars only, may easily follow the inquiry and judge of the results. There has also been present a strong feeling as to the inutility of writing on such subjects in a solemn, or formal, and uninteresting fashion.

All this may suggest the thought of intention outrunning capacity. But, in any case, I hope to be credited with a sincere desire to be of service; and should my reading of Biblical ideas on the nature of God and the destiny of man prove to be correct, the design will be accomplished.

H. H. VOWLES.

GLOUCESTER, *February*, 1898.

CONTENTS

CHAPTER I.
INTRODUCTORY 1   PAGE

The aid of De Quincey invoked that we may be encouraged onward. *Pointless* pointed Hebrew. Rules for Bible reading. The Revised Version's suspicion of For ever and ever, and of its own substitute.

CHAPTER II.
AD 15

This little word set up to tell of Eternity, and thirty other things, confesses its inability to do so.

CHAPTER III.
AD, WITH ADDITIONS 30

What *ad* has to say in the *adys* of souls and women; and in *moads*, such as the moon, the Tabernacle, and the grave.

CHAPTER IV.
AD, AS "CONGREGATION" 40

Rescued from the Whole Congregation, *ad* shows its meaning in a swarm of bees, and in the congregations of the righteous and the hypocrites.

CHAPTER V.
AD, AS "WITNESS" 50

ad comes to its own in the *ads* with which Moses filled heaven and earth, and in the greatest *ads* of the Old and New Testaments.

CHAPTER VI.
OLAM 63

Under examination *olam* contradicts several learned persons, and refuses to have anything to do with Duration, whether long or short.

CHAPTER VII.

OLAM, AS FIXITY 76

The shore claimed by *olam* but not the sea. The leprosy of Gehazi, and some other matters, *olamic* but not everlasting.

CHAPTER VIII.

OLAM, AS INVIOLABILITY AND INEVITABLENESS . . 87

Fixities many, salvation, betrothal, a lady, the grave, life, smoke, anger, deserts, dens, landmarks, and kindness; but none of them eternal save by logical inference.

CHAPTER IX.

THE *OLAM* GOD 102

Glory of *olam* manifestations; and of the *olam* God, as sung by three Hebrew and three English poets.

CHAPTER X.

NEW TESTAMENT 119

How it happens that *olam* appears, in English dress, in a robbed and wounded condition.

CHAPTER XI.

AIŌN 137

Liddell and Scott *versus* Plato, Aristotle, Bishop Westcott, St. Paul, St. Peter, the angel Gabriel, and St. John.

CHAPTER XII.

AIŌN, AS "WORLD" AND "AGE" 154

Seeing the Revisers unable to be happy with either, we turn to Fixity.

CHAPTER XIII.

AIŌNIOS 169

Startled by such an arrant contradiction as Eternal Times, we ask *aiōnios* what it tries to say. The answer seems satisfactory.

CHAPTER XIV.

"ETERNAL LIFE" 186

The thought of endless existence replaced by the bringing in of a better hope.

CHAPTER XV.

"EVERLASTING PUNISHMENT" 210

    Inevitable Restraint; Inevitable Displacement; Inveterate Sin; and Irresistible Fire.

CHAPTER XVI.

CONCLUSION 229

    Ever-during consequences of sin. The doctrine of eternal punishment, as formerly defined, based on exaggerations of stern texts. Everlasting sin and annihilation theories apparently in conflict with belief in omnipotence, and with "the fixed and determinate sense" of Biblical statements.

INDEX 256

How much we gain if we allow words to have their full and proper meaning. For instance: A Seer cannot see what has no existence; and a Revelation cannot be also a mystery, or something incapable of proof.—*Anon.*

"FOR EVER AND EVER."

CHAPTER I.

INTRODUCTORY

THE method and principles of interpretation adopted in this book seem to require a few preliminary observations, despite the probability that some readers, having scanned them, will not think it worth their while to accompany me farther.

In the first place, the writer, with no pretension to an accurate acquaintance with Hebrew and Greek, has yet ventured to think himself competent to pursue an inquiry in regions usually deemed inaccessible except to the profoundest scholarship; and he has furthermore convinced himself that any person of ordinary intelligence is able, although he may have no knowledge whatever of the original tongues, to follow the track here marked out, and estimate the worth of the conclusions reached.

He imagines himself to have found support for this opinion, and no doubt it will be felt that support is needed, in the following words of De Quincey, whose capacity for judgment on such a question will be generally acknowledged :—

"As the reading public and the thinking public is every year outgrowing more and more notoriously the mere learned public, it becomes every year more and more the right of the former public to give the law preferably to the latter public upon all points which concern its own separate interests. In past generations no pains were taken to make explanations that were not called for by the *learned* public. All other readers were ignored. They formed a mob for whom no provision was made. And yet any sensible man, let him be as supercilious as he may, must, on consideration, allow that amongst the crowd of unlearned or half-learned readers who have had neither time nor opportunities for what is called erudition or learned studies, there must always lurk a proportion of men that, by constitution of mind and by the bounty of Nature, are much better fitted for thinking, originally more philosophic and more capaciously endowed than those who are, by accident of position, more learned. Such a natural superiority certainly takes precedence of a merely artificial superiority; and therefore it entitles those who possess it to a special consideration."*

The quotation has been given with a good deal of reluctance because of the implication it appears to involve that the present writer claims for himself, and suggests to his readers that they also may share, some part of that bounty of Nature of which De Quincey speaks. But if any of us should think so, and should even be warranted in so thinking, we must not forget that an accidental possession gives no man the right to glory.

Passing to another topic, if the reader has never spent

* *Expositor*, 1st Series, vii., 406.

INTRODUCTORY.   3

two or three minutes in looking at a Hebrew Bible, he is entreated to do so at once. Supposing him to comply with this counsel, let him turn to the title-page, which he must look for at what we call the end of the book, and examine the characters printed there. He will soon find himself beginning to admire them, and their clearness and stateliness will grow upon him the more he studies them. But, unless I mistake, he will not like them quite so well when in other parts of the volume he sees them all peppered about with tiny dots and strokes, and curves and crosses. These are the Vowel Points and the Accents. I give them the honour of capital letters, for books have been written about them and battles fought. History records that at least one great authority declared them to be inspired. And in our time it seems not a few good and learned men would well-nigh shiver with apprehension at any thought of their removal. Yet it is a simple fact that they are a modern innovation, and that they were invented and brought into use by the descendants and followers of those who were so ignorant of their own Scriptures as not to recognize Him of whom Moses in the law, and the prophets, did write.

Some hundreds of years before Philip spoke the words I have just quoted, the Hebrew Scriptures were translated into Greek. It is important to bear in mind that this Version, called the Septuagint, was in common use in Philip's time, and that the New Testament writers often refer to it. This is especially the case with the author of the Epistle to the Hebrews, whose work, as its title may indicate, will prove of immense value for our present inquiry. A curious parallel might be drawn between the history of the Septuagint, and its fate among men, and that of the Bible itself. There was a time when, as with the Bible, every letter was thought to be supernaturally inspired; so much so, that it was gravely told how, when the seventy-two translators brought in the work, which they had done separately and in guarded seclusion, all the versions were found to agree down to the minutest detail. Later, again like the Bible, it was treated with suspicion; later still with contempt. Now there are plentiful indications that the true value of both is about to be fully seen and appreciated. We shall find this venerable Version of much service to us as we go along. But the thing to remember just now is that the translation of the Scriptures accepted and used by Jesus and His disciples was made from unpointed Hebrew.

A writer in a magazine the other day bestowed a benediction on the inventors of the points because, so he says, without their aid he could never have known whether *dbr* meant a speech or a pestilence. Poor man! Why, instead of falling down and worshipping at the fiat of this point-making Nebuchadnezzar, could he not have studied *dbr* for himself until it yielded up its secret? How did young Saul of Tarsus, sitting at the feet of Gamaliel, learn what *dbr* meant? We may say Gamaliel taught him, and that someone else taught Gamaliel. Still, it is the fact that the teachers taught and the pupils learned without any help from the points.

This is a matter of so much moment that the reader must be asked to look a little longer at *dbr*, or at some other Hebrew word. And this opportunity may be taken of saying that only English characters will be used in

INTRODUCTORY. 5

these pages. They are easier for the writer and for such readers as he hopes to have. And there are those whom the appearance of Hebrew or Greek letters frightens from the perusal of the English in which they are inserted.

In order that we may see what the dots and crosses can make of Hebrew words, we will take, instead of *dbr*, an interesting group like *sd*, *sdh*, *sdy*, and *sdd*. Commonsense, always the best interpreter, would surely suggest to us that these four words, or sets of signs, seeing they are so much alike, must have something in common as to their meaning, and that the terminal characters speak of some particular modification of a general thought. One thinks inscriptions on old-world monuments could never have been deciphered if the same signs had been used to express ideas as much opposed to each other as long and short, and black and white. Let us suppose *sd* and its kindred to occur on one of these, and that, some two thousand years or so after it was chiselled, a man came along with a red pencil and told us we could not understand *sd* until he made a few strokes and dots about it. If he put a mark *here sd* would mean Soil ; if he placed it *there* the significance would be Spoil. Another alteration and addition, and we should have Field or Destruction, as the case might be. As if this were not enough, a further manipulation of the red pencil would give us Desolation, and its opposite, that wonder of creation, a woman's Breast. And, finally, by this magical process of his, he would turn *sd* first into God and then into the Devil ! What should we incline to say to him ? Confound your impudence ?

But this is a true account of the effect produced upon *sd* and its companions by the use of the vowel points. And all has not been said. If we take it that the points are right when they tell us to say Breast or God, they leave us altogether in the dark as to the nature of the God or the quality of the Breast to which they direct us. This they do because they take no account of, and at the same time prevent us from seeing, the thought which is common to the group of words in question. The Hebrew seers did not write like that. They were figurative and picturesque, but, none the less, they were definite and clear.

And if we take the common idea in the four kindred words to be that of Productiveness or Supply, we shall see this. *sd* is used of Soil and Field because they are productive. And Spoil may be viewed as a kind of *enforced* supply; and to that conclusion the terminal letter in *sdd*, judging from similar cases, would direct us. Thinking of the Breast we have no difficulty in seeing what particular and most needful characteristic it is upon which *sd* fixes our attention. And turning to God, we have not now a word without meaning, or with only such a meaning as we, who are not seers, may have put into it, but a most beautiful and helpful illustration—I am the Supreme Supply; walk before Me, and thou wilt be complete. But then the antithesis of Supply, like Desolation or Destruction, cannot properly represent the drift of *sd*. And as to Devils, the translation is ludicrously erroneous. Moses did not accuse his people of sacrificing to Devils, but to "Supplies" that were not Supreme—to idols, in fact, whose breasts, being of wood or metal or stone, were not satisfactory and satisfying.

But if we allow ourselves to be led by the adherents of Jews who did not know their own Scriptures, and who by the sprinkling of dots and strokes, and curves and crosses, have thickened the veil which is on their heart when Moses is read, we shall miss all this, and shall see nothing clearly. It is not in this way that a young Timothy may know the sacred writings, or an Apollos become mighty in the Scriptures. What can be said of the points, then, but that they are interloping mystificators—meddlesome little Scribes and Pharisees, making the Word of God of none effect by their tradition.

It is as the result of this line of thought and observation that the following canon of interpretation has been adopted here:—

No Hebrew character or group of characters had originally and generally more than one meaning; and two Hebrew words were never used to express the same idea.

Very probably a more perfect acquaintance with the Hebrew tongue would show that the rule has exceptions; but whether I am right or not in allowing it to influence me, almost every page of this book will afford materials for judging.

Another governing thought has been the persuasion that the larger part of the Bible is revelation; and revelation is taken to imply the bringing of a thing into our knowledge. But how can we be said to *know* a thing if it be in all ways impossible of proof? In other words, the Hebrew prophets did not speak words and sentences that have no definite meaning; and they were not Agnostics— they did not speak of the unknowable. When, therefore, in our English Versions a prophet or an apostle is represented as talking in a way not lucid, or as professing to make known things which are not in some possible way capable of demonstration, the "translation" is to be suspected of inaccuracy. This, as will be seen, is only another way of saying that more reverence is felt for prophets and apostles than for their interpreters.

When any would-be interpreter of Scripture gives a meaning to Biblical words and phrases without setting forth, for the judgment of the competent, the method of his investigation and the reasons for his conclusions, he is in danger of doing a great deal of harm. His work will have the appearance of dogmatism, if not of infallibility, very hurtful to it in the eyes of the discriminating. He will run the risk of encouraging those whose mental indolence is only too ready to accept "beliefs" at second hand. And he may get himself into such a condition of mind as to pain some honest inquirer, who challenges his conclusions, by showing that uncharitableness and other horrid things may exist in unexpected quarters. It is sincerely hoped in the present case to avoid these evils. I do not believe For ever and ever, or For ever singly, to give a correct account of Biblical phraseology any more than I can accept Pitch and Purge as true renderings of one Hebrew word. Such translations are put forth with authority, and declared to be true, *without evidence offered.*

Let me say, as the last of these preliminary words, that my desire is to take the reader with me in every step. If sometimes we seem to stray from the path leading onward to some adequate conception of what the Bible means by "Eternal Life" and "Everlasting Punishment," it is only that by the way we may increase our knowledge of the Bible generally. To this end, and because people do not ordinarily carry Bibles about with them, and are not always to be trusted to refer to them when they have them at their elbow, the texts of Scripture will be given fully and with prominence. By this and other means every opportunity will be afforded him who reads for weighing the worth of what may be advanced. When we reach the end perhaps we shall resolve to dwell together as partners in faith. If not, we will either say good-bye in friendly fashion, or set to work and fight each other (with the gloves on), just as the reader shall choose.

This introductory chapter may be completed by considering how the phrase For ever and ever looks in the light of the rules, of which an account has been given. And first of all let us ask, Is it clear? It is familiar; no phrase more so. We use it in repeating the Lord's Prayer; and many of us, whether Churchmen, Wesleyans, or Dissenters, are probably unaware that in this particular instance we owe the repetition of the Ever, not to the Bible, but to the Prayer Book. But which of us is able to say definitely what is meant by it? Is there any difference in duration between For ever and For ever and ever? One writer says there is. In his opinion the first Ever points to the former eternity, and the second to the eternity still to come. But St. John has a text which puts that theory out of court:—

Rev. xix. 3. And her smoke rose up for ever and ever.

This quotation affords a striking example of what has been said of cases in which the correctness of the rendering is to be suspected. How could a man say what he is here represented as saying? For he depicts himself as finding a point of view at the end of eternity! and looking back from it he says, Her smoke rose up for ever and ever. The revisers say, Her smoke *goeth* up for ever and ever. But the fitting tense to use in such a statement is the future, Her smoke *shall* go up. The use of the present tense goes to show that St. John was speaking of a quality evidently present. But that quality could not be unending duration, for that is in the future, and so far as smoke is concerned, not open to proof.

A more important passage will afford opportunity for the application of another rule. Its value for our purpose is that it is found in both Old and New Testaments:—

Heb. i. 8. Thy throne, O God, is for ever and ever.
Ps. xlv. 6.

No objection could be raised here, at least to what the English says to us, if we take the text as it stands, and do not trouble about the unmeaning repetition. To a Hebrew Jehovah was the chief of certainties, or he would have no warrant for saying, O fear Jehovah ye His saints, for there is no want to them that fear Him. And he would have no difficulty in proving that the Supreme must be eternal. And yet I am not aware of any text in which the Hebrew and Greek words about to be mentioned directly attribute eternity even to God; though there are many where they speak of another and greater and more comprehensive quality, from the possession of which His eternity may logically be argued. And I say this knowing that the words in question are almost the only words which in our version are represented by For ever and its equivalents;

so careful, as it seems to me, were the Bible writers not to advance anything that might be questioned as wanting in clearness and demonstrableness. Bishop Westcott, however, in his commentary on the Epistle, says the text is to be read, God is thy throne for ever and ever. In that case much the same difficulties would confront us as in the text about the smoke.

But, leaving this, let us see what comes of the fact that these words, occurring in an Epistle to Hebrew people, are quoted from a Hebrew Psalm. Now the reader may never have seen a Hebrew or a Greek word in his life, but he is, nevertheless, entreated to believe himself quite able to understand what follows. In the English we have the repetition of a word, and the reader, as he looks at Ever Ever, knows that he has the same word before him printed twice. What the translators turned into Ever Ever appears in the Greek of the Epistle as—omitting case-endings—*aiōn aiōn*. Once more the reader will see that he has two words before him which in appearance are exactly alike, and he will guess, and rightly so, that they are identical in meaning. And now he will be interested in looking at the words in the Hebrew Psalm. They are *olam ad*. Anyone seeing them will say they are not at all similar, and will find it hard to believe that they both signify just the same thing. And this is the conclusion to which a part of one of the rules of interpretation leads us. If *olam* means eternal, then *ad* stands for something else; if *ad* is the sign for endless duration, then *olam* must have another significance.

It is manifest there is something wrong. If there be any truth in the theory now under notice the fault must lie between the writer of the Epistle, or that ancient Greek

Version from which he probably copied, and the makers of the English Translation. It will most certainly be said without hesitation that the theory is wrong. And, seeing what is on one side and what on the other, who can wonder?

There is, however, a remarkable fact that has not yet come into evidence. The English Version has been revised. The revisers were a company of the greatest scholars of the age. And they were a most conservative body, restrained by injunction, as well as by taste and inclination, from making any change except when required to do so by faithfulness to the original. Knowing all this, we may be quite sure it would be with the greatest possible reluctance that they would touch such a sentence as For ever and ever; so "sonorous and rhythmical" is it, so familiar, and so common in devotional use. Nor have they altered it in the text; a majority of not less than two-thirds would have been necessary for that. But in most places where the phrase occurs they have put in the margin, *Greek:* Unto the ages of the ages. This tells us that faithfulness to the original demanded that some token should be given of the fact that For ever and ever is not an exact translation. And the marginal note says plainly that the original words do not mean eternity. For Unto the ages of the ages, whatever significance imagination or assertion may fix upon it, does not, like For ever and ever, unmistakably set forth the thought of never-ending duration. So that no less an authority than the Revised Version casts doubt upon the right of Ever Ever to represent *aiōn aiōn* and *olam ad.*

But this is not all. It has just been said the revisers

put the marginal note in most places where For ever and ever occurs, not in all. An exception is found in the case of the text which has been quoted from the Epistle to Hebrews. Why is the marginal note omitted there? There can be no reason, save that in this instance *aiōn aiōn* is in the singular number, and had the revisers put their correction in the margin it must have been in the form of Unto the age of the age. And the studious reader will find that the rule apparently followed has been this: When *aiōn* is found in the plural number, let the note, correcting For ever, be Unto the ages; but when *aiōn* is singular, let For ever stand unchallenged. Thus we have a strange result—the singular number denotes eternity, but the plural number something not so long! But, as we all know, alteration in number does not imply alteration in nature; and the point to fix our eyes on is that the work of the revisers having shown dissatisfaction with the rendering of their predecessors, cannot conceal their dissatisfaction with their own alternative.

Is it any wonder if they did feel like that? Thy throne, O God, is unto the age of the age: He shall reign unto the ages: Shall not die unto the age. Let it be asked seriously, What do such expressions mean? Are they revelation? If so, what do they bring into knowledge? What language is, Unto the ages of the ages? Classical Greek scholars assure me it is not Greek, as known to them. We can all see it is not English. English people do not talk like that, and cannot understand people who do. As a matter of fact, Unto the ages of the ages looks like what Matthew Arnold would call words thrown out at an object imperfectly understood.

So the search for error is somewhat cunningly turned aside from our theory; for even though the hunter should be right in condemning it, he is still left with this dilemma: either something is wrong with the versions, or the Bible, the Word of God, uses on the most momentous subjects language which is vague, pointless, and unverifiable.

As I said before, we ought to have more reverence for the Bible than for its translators and its commentators. But we shall probably come to the conclusion by-and-by that the fault is not so much with the versions as with the forgetfulness of the fact that the New Testament was written by Jews, and that they wrote as they did because, unlike Scribes and Pharisees, they had come to understand the Hebrew Scriptures.

If we admit they wrote about religion in the Greek as we possess it, still it is not to be denied they thought in Hebrew, and that Hebrew peculiarities of idea and diction governed their use of the Greek language. And this would be true, even though it should turn out that their acquaintance with Hebrew thought came to them only through the ancient Greek Version. But it follows from this fact that the most efficient help towards the comprehension of their writings is not a Greek lexicon and familiarity with Greek authors, but a knowledge of the Hebrew Scriptures. Had this inference been allowed its proper weight, the revisers, instead of putting into the margin of their work, *Greek:* Unto the ages of the ages, would rather have written, *Hebrew:* ———. What they may perhaps have written there it is the business of our succeeding chapters to discover.

CHAPTER II.

AD

ad is something like a guide-post which has been also used as a clothes-horse, or as a target for the missiles of schoolboys, and even as a gallows, but whose only power to help the wayfarer is in its original intention.

IT is to be feared that some people merely glancing at the pages of this chapter may think they have little or nothing presented to them but lists of Biblical passages. And there is no denying that texts of Scripture are very often dry and void of interest both in themselves, as seen by us in English dress, and in the setting sometimes given them.

There is, however, no insuperable reason for this. The Bible is really the most fascinating of books, when the veil so often hiding its beauty is taken away. And in this search of ours there will be plenty of amusement, to say nothing of anything more worthy, for all who are willing to join.

Our present business is with *ad*, the less important of the two Hebrew words taken to imply endless duration. And we have first to ask if it will bear that meaning.

Here is a text where *ad* (in this sense) seems to be at home:—

Isa. lvii. 15. The high and lofty One that inhabiteth *ad* (eternity).

But in the next instance the English word is beyond doubt an intruder:—

Hab. iii. 6. The *ad* (everlasting) mountains were scattered.

Mountains are not everlasting; and if they were they could not be scattered. But I will cite two cases in which the use of *ad* in the sense supposed is quite impossible even to poetical and figurative speech, and the translators have been obliged to employ other words.

Gen. xlix. 27. Benjamin is a wolf that ravineth:
In the morning he shall devour the *ad* (prey),
And at even he shall divide the spoil.

Job xvi. 7. Thou hast made desolate all my *ad* (company).

On our hypothesis these four examples are sufficient to settle the question; for the same Hebrew word is made to speak of different things, and things as diverse as Eternity, Prey, and Company. And seeing there are other terms in Hebrew to express these, the employment of *ad* to represent them is contrary to that other part of the rule which says two Hebrew words are not used to set forth the same thought. Then something has been said about want of clearness being a sign of imperfect translation. Does the third example convey a distinct meaning? If a wolf devours the Prey, say a goose or a kid, in the morning, how is he to divide the spoil in the evening?—unless, indeed, we think of the spoil as the feathers or the fur remaining after the feast. Evidently Prey cannot be the meaning of *ad* in this ancient scrap of poetry; and the substitution for Prey of either of the other words, Eternity or Company, will not make the matter clearer. The wolf, or Benjamin, could not devour Eternity; and if he devoured his Company, with whom could he divide the Spoil?

While we are in this mood we may as well say a word or two about that other notion as to the sayings of seers being capable of demonstration. Let us recall a verse which will suit our purpose better than any of the four just recorded. David is represented as saying to Solomon:—

1 *Chron.* xxviii. 9. If thou forsake Him He will cast thee off *ad* (for ever).

That David had in him the gift or vision of a seer will not be questioned. But seers do not, and cannot, see what David is represented as saying in this verse. Not to dwell on the fact that David had himself, at times, "forsaken" God and had not been cast off for ever, when could he or anyone know that God had cast a man off for *ever?* The only possible answer is, when the Ever came to an end, and that is *Never.* One has too much respect for David to think that he would say, and in such solemn circumstances, what he did not know, and the inevitable conclusion is that *ad* does not mean For ever.

And now perhaps enough has been said on the negative side. Destructive criticism—taking off one's coat to pull down other men's work—is sometimes necessary. But a true critic does not stop there; nay, it may be said he does not begin there unless he imagines himself to have something better to put in its place. What has to be done here is to furnish a translation of *ad* that will fit every one of the instances of its use, or misuse, already given. And not these alone. For, with slight additions by way of prefix or suffix, *ad* is set up to represent, as best it may, Witness, Congregation, Mouth, Ornament, Appointed Time, Solemnity, and Tent of Meeting. And more than these, for there is a very wide prepositional use of the word inclusive of such terms as To, Until, Against, Before, While, By, and Both.

Reviewing this long and varied list, it seems preposterous to say that *ad* originally had but one meaning, and that reference to the places where the English words in the catalogue just given occur will prove the truth of the statement; but this is the task before us. Knowing something of the evidence, it may be said, in language used at a celebrated trial, "We propose to show, not only that the claimant is not the person he has been supposed to be, but also who he really is, and that he cannot be anybody else."

The opinion, then, put forth here is that *ad* is the Hebrew sign for Prominence, and for that alone.

Before adducing the evidence a word must be said as to the passages to be cited. It would swell this book beyond reasonable proportions to quote every instance of the use of *ad*. But the reader may take the assurance that every important passage is reproduced and submitted for his scrutiny. Particularly may he be certain that this is so with the instances in which *ad* is rendered by English terms expressive of perpetuity. And as it is our main purpose to show that the use of such terms is unwarranted and misleading, we may as well begin with the texts in which they are found.

We have For ever as representing *ad* in many places. I will give three, which have been selected as illustrative of classes into which these many texts might be divided. Some others in which *ad* is linked with *olam* will come up for discussion later.

One instance of the use of For ever we have met with already in the words of David to Solomon. And it was objected that David could not know what the English Bible makes him say. But there is no difficulty in seeing that he is really speaking of a *prominent* "casting off." It was Solomon, the young man of splendid parts and magnificent opportunities, to whom the aged king is saying, If *thou* forsake Him the "casting off" will not be an ordinary one! And this interpretation strikingly accords with the subsequent history.

An example of a different kind is taken from one of the Psalms:—

Psalm xxi. 6.   Thou hast made him most blessed for ever.

The revisers have recognized the impossibility of such a reading, and they substitute, Thou makest him most blessed for ever. But this does not do away with the unlikelihood of the ascription, except by parasites and flatterers, of everlasting blessedness to a king who is still exposed to the vicissitudes of earth. A seer would not say that; but it would be quite within his vocation to call attention to the fact that the king was being *prominently* blessed, and this is just what he does.

And Prominence seems to be the chief thought in what Job says about what is sometimes called his inscription:—

Job xix. 23, 24.   Oh that my words were now written!
Oh that they were printed in a book!
That with an iron pen and lead
They were graven in the rock for ever!

Did he wish the words of his inscription, so familiar to us as "I know that my Redeemer liveth," to endure for ever and ever? Perhaps he did. But the primary aspiration is evidently for writing, printing, chiselling in the rock, *i.e.*, for *publication*. He would not keep what he feels and knows hidden in his heart; he would have it set in tablets before the eyes of the learned, and cut upon the face of the cliff, so that he who ran might read.

There are other words having the notion of everlastingness doing duty in our Version as representatives of *ad*. These are Perpetually, Eternity, and Everlasting.

The first occurs in the prophecy of Amos.

Amos i. 11. His anger did tear perpetually, and he kept his wrath for ever.

In this verse For ever takes the place of a Hebrew word meaning Continuance, and *ad* is turned into Perpetually. The idea that *ad* must mean Duration is accountable for making the prophet appear to say the same thing twice over. But he is much better understood if we read him as declaring the anger of Edom to have been both prominent and continuous.

We have had an instance of Everlasting in a passage from Habakkuk. Mountains are not eternal, but they are prominent—incontestably so. And this, too, would seem to be the drift of *ad* in the only other place where it is translated Everlasting.

Isaiah ix. 6. His name shall be called Wonderful, Counsellor, Mighty God, Father *ad*, Prince of Peace.

Here our word appears to be used to give prominence to the Fatherliness of the coming Ruler; it is as though we were to say His character, or the character of His government, will be eminently paternal.

The only place in which Eternity appears as synonymous with *ad* has already been glanced at. Quoted in full, it reads:—

Isaiah lvii. 15. Thus saith the high and lofty One that inhabiteth eternity, whose name is Holy; I dwell in the high and holy place, with him also that is of a contrite and humble spirit.

Is it mere cavilling to say that "inhabiteth eternity" is not revelation? No need for a seer to tell men this. But suppose we read *inhabiteth prominently*. We are then led to ask, Where? And the text furnishes the answer. Not only in the temple doth Jehovah dwell—few Jews needed to be reminded of that; but also, and quite as prominently, with the contrite and humble spirit. And this is indeed a truth many Jews, and not they only, need seers to see for them and proclaim to them.

Thus it would seem that in those very places where the notion of Endless Duration is, at first sight, not unsuitable, the idea of Prominence affords a preferable meaning; and were these the only instances of the occurrence of *ad* in the Old Testament, it might be argued from them alone that Prominence and not Everlastingness is its true meaning. But when we turn to those cases in which the idea of Eternity is impossible, and where the words employed by the translators actually confuse the sense, while the thought of Prominence gives a clear and definite meaning, the argument becomes unanswerable.

The reader will recall an instance in which *ad* was turned into Prey, and another when it was said to be

Company. Let us see what support they render our theory. The difficulty in the way of our understanding the prediction about Benjamin arises partly from the strange translation of *ad* into Prey, and partly from the use of the word Devour. Nowadays we only devour with our eating apparatus, but in the Bible we often find men "devouring" with fire and sword. If we remember this, and at the same time bear in mind the true meaning of *ad*, the perplexity with which we view the text as it stands in our Bible will vanish. The Prominences between Benjamin and the spoil were the obstacles and difficulties naturally to be thought of in such a connection, and his father pictures him as overcoming these in the morning and then in the evening dividing the spoil.

The quotation from the Book of Job is specially interesting and, I may add, convincing :—

Job xvi. 7-8. Thou hast made desolate all my *ad* (company) ; and thou hast filled me with wrinkles which is a *ad* (witness) against me.

Here it is to be noted, first, that "which is" and "against me" have nothing answering to them in the original; and, secondly, that our word *ad* occurs twice. The translators have rendered it by Witness in obedience to the point-makers, and they have, in consequence, felt themselves obliged to add "which is" and "against me" to make any sense at all. But, even so, what sense there is seems misleading. Restoring the true meaning of *ad* in both places, the text will strike everyone by its pathetic force and beauty. Before his affliction, Job's prosperity, peace, and happiness were prominent indeed. Now they are all "made desolate." And not without a touch of gloomy irony, alluding either to his trouble-wrinkled brow or, more probably, to the corrugations on his skin, which were one of the characteristics of his disease, he complains:—

Thou hast made desolate all my eminence;
And thou hast given me wrinkles for eminence!

But there is still what I may call a stronghold of the enemy which must be assailed and, if it may be, conquered, or readers may differ even yet as to the victorious opinion. It has been remarked that *ad* is very widely used as a preposition. Now it is said Hebrew prepositions were, once upon a time, all of them substantives, and among them *ad* was a substantive denoting, not Endlessness, but Duration simply; the everlasting character of the duration was brought in as circumstances seemed to call for it.

The reader must note that this is mere conjecture, as much in the case of the shorter as in that of the longer duration-sense imposed upon *ad*. But, taking the word to mean this, scholars have said that *ad* in its prepositional use must be translated by English words significant of Duration, such as Until, While, So long as, and Till. Now this is the position we are to attack, and capture if we can.

No one will deny that the assertion to be combated has, at first survey, a look of impregnability about it. I will give an instance of the use of each of the four English prepositions just enumerated, and the reader will see how difficult it would be to replace them by words not having the purport of duration.

Numbers xxxii. 13. And the Lord's anger was kindled against Israel, and He made them wander to and fro in the wilderness forty years, *ad* (until) all the generation that had done evil in the sight of the Lord was consumed.

Judges iii. 26. And Ehud escaped *ad* (while) they tarried.

2 *Kings* ix. 22. And he answered, What peace *ad* (so long as) the whoredoms of thy mother Jezebel and her witchcrafts are so many?

Job xiv. 14. All the days of my appointed time will I wait *ad* (till) my change come.

As was intimated, it is not an easy matter to change these words for others not having a duration-sense. Nor is it suggested that such a course should be adopted. The translation is as perfect, probably, as English words can make it. Nevertheless, the thought present in *ad* in all these cases is not that of duration but of prominence, and the expression of this, if it could be managed, would make the texts much more graphic.

The fact is, *ad* is used in these examples much as we use a ☞. Its business is to call attention to, or make prominent, some particular circumstance. If in a text or two we turn *ad* into a ☞ this will be clear.

Ezekiel iii. 13. The people shouted with a loud shout, and the noise was heard——☞ afar off!

Exodus xxxiii. 22. I will put thee in a cleft of the rock . . . and I will cover thee with my hand——☞ I pass by!

In the first of these instances no English preposition is needed, and a duration-signifying one is inadmissible, but the reader sees at a glance what it is that *ad* is set to do. In the second, the English preposition While lays stress upon the time occupied in the passing rather than upon he passing itself. But *ad* is employed to emphasize this latter thought, and the effect is as though we underscored the words *I pass by*.

Reading the four texts given as illustrations in this way, we see how in the first *ad* makes conspicuous the fact that all the generation guilty of evil perished. In the text from Judges *ad's* finger points to the tarrying of the servants as Ehud's opportunity for escaping. The question of Jehu is much more pointed when we recognize the exact force of our word.

What, *Peace!* ☞ The many whoredoms of thy mother Jezebel, and her witchcrafts!

Job's words, taken with the context, seem to have this meaning: If a man die shall he live again? If so, I would wait with patience all the days of my appointed time. Yes! with patience——☞ my change would come!

The assertion, then, that *ad* requires a duration-preposition to translate it turns out to be not so incontrovertible as it appeared. As we proceed we shall find it less and less so. And before long we shall discover instances of the prepositional use of our acquaintance, for so we may now call *ad*, where any thought of duration is altogether out of the question.

I will give two or three texts in which the sense of Prominence is, to say the least, preferable to the sense of Duration, and, it may be added, they are fair samples of a multitude that might be adduced.

Genesis xiii. 12. And Lot dwelled in the cities of the plain, and pitched his tent——☞ Sodom!

Exodus xxii. 26. If thou at all take thy neighbour's garment in pledge, thou shalt restore it to him——☞ the sun goeth down, and that is his only garment.

Job xx. 4. 5. Knowest thou not this of old time,
Since man was placed upon the earth :
That the triumphing of the wicked is short,
And the joy of the godless —— ☞ a moment !

Putting the drift of these quotations into other words, we may say, Lot pitched his tent where Sodom and its wickedness was conspicuous. Take thy neighbour's cloak in pledge if thou wilt, but keep this fact prominently before thee: The sun goeth down, and the cloak is his only covering. The joy of wickedness may be great, but how prominent is the truth that it is only momentary!

The end of this chapter is in sight. But two or three instances of the use of *ad* were promised in which the utmost ingenuity could not give it the sense of Duration. Here they are, and if only three are given it is out of consideration for the reader's patience.

Numbers viii. 4. And this was the work of the candlestick, beaten work of gold ; *ad* the base thereof, and *ad* the flowers thereof, it was beaten work.

As I said, it is not possible to bring in the duration meaning here. From another place we learn that every part of the candlestick was of gold. In the text just quoted *ad* is employed to give prominence to that fact by pointing to both "base" and "flowers," or all that springs from the base, as being of the same precious metal.

Judges xx. 48. And the men of Israel turned again upon the children of Benjamin, and smote them with the edge of the sword, *ad* the entire city, and the cattle, and all that they found.

The A.V. reads: As well the men of every city as the beast. The R.V. changes this to: Both the entire city and the cattle. Either account is correct and conveys the sense. But, as we can all see, the work of *ad* is to call into prominence the fact that both men and cattle were smitten by the sword.

The last example is :—

1 *Chronicles* iv. 27. Neither did all their family multiply *ad* the children of Judah.

This instance is curiously interesting. The former part of the verse refers to the descendants of Simeon, and hints that they were not very numerous. Then *ad* is brought in to point to the children of Judah. Why? Because the historian has just been enumerating the progeny of Judah, and, compared with the children of Simeon, their name was legion. So that while the English Bible very properly says, Like to the children of Judah, we cannot but once again recognize the fact that the duty assigned to *ad* is, here as in the other citations, to make things conspicuous.

We may now take leave of *ad*, in its simple form, for the present. We have pursued it in many directions and scrutinized it in many situations, and the result is that in the text which was our starting-point,

Thy throne, O God, is *olam ad*,

whatever may turn out to be the case with *olam*, that other Hebrew word, *ad*, is not a Hebrew equivalent for Eternity, but is, in some way, the sign for Prominence.

CHAPTER III.

AD, WITH ADDITIONS.

If one were to say, That stable has a cow in it, not a horse ; I am the stable-keeper, and you must take it on my authority, what man of sense would heed him ? In these pages it is maintained that the stable contains a horse, but all who are interested are invited to take the key and see for themselves.

THIS chapter, as its title indicates, will be devoted to an account of the use of *ad* in combination with other letters whose presence, while indicating some modification or particular application of the main thought, does not at all affect the primary meaning of the word. That this is so will be evident as we go along, and thus further proof will offer itself to support our theory.

The first of the forms to be considered may be set down here as *ady*.

Our translators have chosen two words to represent it, so dissimilar, and so unlike anything we have hitherto met with in our reading of *ad*, that we shall not be surprised to find every passage in which they occur more or less wanting in clearness. The words are Mouth and Ornament. Now on the principle advocated Mouth and Ornament ought to be convertible terms. But are they so always ? It is true, both may be suggestive of Prominence, but neither is that invariably the case. This fact, and the foregoing chapter, will probably have prepared us for the discovery that neither word is to be trusted to give a true account of *ady's* meaning.

Two texts may be given in which Mouth might perhaps, but for what we have seen, pass without raising suspicion as to its capacity.

Psalm xxxii. 9. Be not ye as the horse, or as the mule, which have no understanding : whose *ady* must be held in with bit and bridle, that they come not near thee.

Psalm ciii. 5. Who satisfieth thy *ady* with good things ;
So that thy youth is renewed like the eagle's.

These may be followed by another in which Mouth could not possibly have place.

Ezekiel vii. 20. As for the beauty of his *ady*, he set it in majesty.

Why could not *ady* be turned into Mouth here as in the other cases? The answer is both startling and amusing. It is because the prophet goes on to say in the same breath, But they made the images of their abominations and their detestable things *therein !* This gives us an idea of the troubles of translators. They could not say Mouth, and so they say Ornament. But how could whoever is spoken of set images of abominations in his ornament? The vagueness of such an assertion is a hint that the right word has not been chosen.

There are other places in which Mouth is unsuitable, The vagaries of feminine adornment have been such, that in the first of the quotations that follow it is not altogether impossible to think of Saul as decorating the daughters of Israel with golden images of the human Mouth. But in the second instance Mouth is not to be thought of for a moment.

2 *Samuel* i. 24. Ye daughters of Israel, weep over Saul,
Who clothed you with scarlet delicately,
Who put *adys* of gold upon your apparel.

Exodus xxxiii. 5. Therefore now put off thy *adys* from thee, that I may know what to do to thee. And the children of Israel stripped themselves of their *adys* from Mount Horeb.

The people certainly did not strip off their Mouths! But if the rule followed and supported so far is to be trusted, the fact that *ady* cannot be truly represented here by Mouth is a proof that mouth is incorrect in other places. Therefore, unlikely as this may seem without further investigation, it must be wrong to read of the horse and the mule, whose *Mouth* must be held in with bit and bridle, and quite as erroneous to report the psalmist as saying, Who satisfieth thy mouth with good things.

And this holds good of the other word, Ornament. It will not fit all the circumstances. We may read, The children of Israel stripped themselves of their ornaments, and so make sense; but we cannot say, Who satisfieth thy ornament with good things. And indeed how is it possible to suppose that with *ad* standing as the sign of Prominence the mere addition of a stroke could make it signify Mouth or Ornament just as the reader might choose? We shall expect to find that in all these texts, and in others yet to be noticed, the thought of Prominence is present. All the modification effected by the terminal letter in *ady* is that it points to the particular Prominence peculiar to the person, or thing, or circumstance under consideration.

One or two sayings of the seers of Israel will help us to see this clearly:—

AD, WITH ADDITIONS. 31

Jeremiah ii. 32. Can a maid forget her *adys*, or a bride her attire? Yet my people have forgotten me days without number.

What are a maid's *adys*? The translators say her ornaments; they might just as well have said her mouth! Bible speakers often repeat a thought in another form, and this is the case in the text before us. After speaking of the maid's *adys*, the prophet mentions the bride's attire; so we may guess that in speaking of a maiden's *adys* he is thinking of something in connection with marriage—that most prominent of all events in a woman's life. Having thought of this, a verse from another prophet will confirm us in the conviction that we are on the right track:—

Ezekiel xvi. 7. I caused thee to multiply as the bud of the field, and thou didst increase and wax great; and thou attainedst unto the *ady* of *adys*.

In the beautiful imagery of these words and their context Israel is likened to a baby maiden. The baby again is likened to a bud. She grows and expands and increases until she attains to the full ripeness of womanhood. Then we read, When I passed by thee, and looked upon thee, behold thy time was the time of love. A maid's *ady*, then, is not Excellent Ornament, as the A.V. has it, nor Ornament of Ornaments, as the R.V. reads, but the dawn of womanhood, and the advent of love and marriage—her most momentous time; in other words, her Prominence of Prominences.

This interpretation fits all the instances of the use of *ady*. It is the Prominence peculiar to the person or thing spoken of. Thus the *ady* peculiar to horse and mule is the energy or vigour which needs to be restrained from unintelligent and inconvenient exhibition. According to the psalmist there are men like that. There are those whom Jehovah guides with His eye. For others He has bit and bridle; and in desperate cases, according to Isaiah, even a hook for the nose.

The quotation from Ezekiel, about setting the beauty of his ornament in majesty, need not detain us. It refers probably to the Temple, that chief of Israel's Prominences, and we shall have enough talk about that later on. But what were the *adys* the men of Israel had to strip off at Horeb? Perhaps really "ornaments," so-called, of gold and silver—rings for ears, noses, fingers, arms, and ankles, and such like. But most certainly not these alone. Something more prominent than these, such as Distrust, Disobedience, Rebellion, and Riotous Mirth. Now they were to be stripped of these and humbled, and Jehovah alone was to be exalted in that day.

In the other quotation from the Psalms, the *ady* is that which is peculiar to the "soul." For the psalmist is speaking to his soul, reminding it, in fact, how great things Jehovah had done for it. And this is the climax, He satisfieth, O my soul, thy *ady* with good. What is the *ady*, or Prominence, peculiar to the soul when full of the thought of God, and the fate of the world, and its own capabilities and destiny? Each reader can answer the question for himself.

Passing to fresh fields of exploration, the new form of *ad*, with additions, to come under our notice may be written as *moad*.

The first two letters of this fresh form represent two

prefixes; and so far as a decipherer of hieroglyphics, rather than a Hebrew scholar, may make out, the first says something like Originated, and the second Supported. Combining the two, we may say, as indeed the English Bible does say in some places, that *moad* means an Appointed *ad*. And so far as I can judge it is only used with reference to things of that kind, such as the Moon, the Tabernacle, the Feasts, and Set Times and Signals. The word is an exceedingly interesting one, and on examination will be found a valuable witness to the truth of our theory.

Let us take a few instances of its use.

Psalm civ. 19. He appointed the moon for *moads*.

The translators say Seasons; but this is not at all clear. What seasons are they for which the moon was appointed? But the acquaintance we have made with *ad* enables us to read the text with apprehension. The moon is an Appointed Prominence for Light, for Tides, and for Navigation. Some people think it is also an Appointed Prominence for the weather. And there was a time, as the word lunatic shows, when all people thought it was something of the sort for mad folks.

Num. ix. 2-3. Let the children of Israel keep the Passover in its *moad* (appointed season). In the fourteenth day of the month at even, ye shall keep it in its *moad* (appointed season); according to all the statutes of it, and according to all the ordinances of it shall ye keep it.

Here again the rendering adopted in our Bible is not competent to express all that is meant by *moad*. The ordered prominences of the Passover comprised much more than the season, or time, chosen for its celebration. The Lamb, the Sprinkling of the Blood, the Feast, the question and answer as to the meaning of the rite were all Appointed Prominences of "the night much to be observed unto the Lord for bringing them out of the land of Egypt."

The exact force of *moad* as distinguished from *ad* is strikingly shown in the following example :—

Judges xx. 38. Now the *moad* (appointed sign) between the men of Israel and the liers in wait was that they should make a great cloud of smoke rise up out of the city.

The cloud of smoke set rising as a signal was a Prominence; and it went up as the result of pre-arrangement and consequent action.

Two more instances of very special interest may be given, and then for the present we shall have done with *moad*.

Isaiah xiv. 13-14. Thou saidst in thine heart, I will ascend into heaven : I will sit upon the mount of *moad* in the uttermost parts of the north : I will ascend above the heights of the clouds ; I will be like the Most High.

The A.V. calls the mount of *moad* the mount of congregation. A perfectly bewildering rendering. The thoughtful reader coming upon it cannot but turn away asking, What did the prophet really say? But he will see, if he looks at the words again, that "mount *moad*" is used as an expression parallel with Heaven, above the stars and the heights of the clouds. The King of Babylon has said in his heart that he will make himself pre-eminently prominent. Nay, he will be like God Himself! Not only *ad*, but *moad*. He will originate and support a sovereignty equal to that of the Deity. But, as the prophet goes on to declare, this may not be : Thou shalt be brought down to Shoel, to the uttermost part of the pit.

The other illustration to which I referred is connected with the Hebrew word for House. It is known generally to Bible readers as *Beth*. Really it is the sign for In. Such a word as Bethel becomes more interesting and helpful when we remember this. It is not necessarily any house or building dedicated to God; there was no building on the spot of which Jacob said, This is none other but the house of God. Bethel is *God-in;* and it is any place, church or moor or human spirit, in which the Supreme is manifestly present.

But, to leave this, let us think of another *Beth* in which, we may dare to say, the Supreme is never present. I speak of *Beth moad*. We know what it is, and recognize the beauty of the expression when we read the passage in which it occurs :—

Job xxx. 23. I know thou wilt bring me to death,
And to the *Beth moad* (house appointed) for all living.

It is the most prominent "house" on this earth. It is *moad* as well as *ad;* determined and sustained until its work is done. Think of the vast procession never ceasing through the ages in its progress there. Think of the stately chambers, the obscure corners, and the noisome cellars. It is the *in* that, some day, will include us all. Notwithstanding, let us be of good cheer; like the throne of God, the grave is *ad;* but, unlike that throne, it is not *olam*.

Another interesting variation of *ad* is *adh*. It is represented in our English Bibles by such a row of varieties as Adah, Testimonies, Take away, Pass, Deck, Adorn, Congregation, and Swarm. How impossible, let me say once more, it seems even to imagine such a congerie of ideas arising in the mind of the ancient reader of *adh*, and demanding his instant choice. The word Congregation, in this connection, seems to lead to so extraordinary a field of pleasing information that we will give it a chapter to itself; and Swarm, being something akin to Congregation (when there is a popular preacher), may go with it.

Adah was a wife (the definite article in this matter was not then in force) of Lamech. One of the wives of Esau also bore the name. What these ancient dames were famous for, or what kind of eminence was shrined in the wishes of those who named them, whether beauty, amiability, or motherhood, history does not record. But if we are right so far, there can be no doubt of the general purport of the name.

As to the terms professing to be translations of *adh*, they are so widely different in meaning, that if I give an example of each it will be sufficient to enable the reader to judge whether, in this branch of our inquiry also, the conclusion already arrived at finds corroboration.

Deut. iv. 45. These are the *adh* (testimonies), and the statutes, and the judgments, which Moses spake unto the children of Israel when they came forth out of Egypt.

Is there any real difference between Testimonies, Statutes, and Judgments? We must either think that there is, or that the Bible speaks in a tautological way which is not altogether edifying. The truth seems to be that the sign translated "and" is better rendered by *of*. In that case we should read, The prominences of the statutes of the judgments. The "judgments" are the decisions upon which the "statutes" which put the judgments into words were based. The prominences in the present instance, as the address of Moses shows, were the promulgation of the statutes and the incidents accompanying it.

To proceed, I will quote a strange proverb from the collection of Solomon, of which a clear and satisfactory rendering into English no man has yet accomplished, and probably never will. Despite this, however, we may glean something even here to reward our search.

Prov. xxv. 20. As one that *adh* (taketh off) his garment in cold weather, and as vinegar upon nitre, so is he that singeth songs to a heavy heart.

"Vinegar upon nitre" is one of the difficulties, and is likely to remain so. The Septuagint has Vinegar upon a *sore*, which is rather good—good sense, I mean, of course. Those far-off translators appear to have had before them some other version of the rest of the proverb. The last clause as we have it should probably run, Singeth songs upon a heavy heart. For the heavy heart to be sung to might be a bore, but would hardly warrant such a comparison as nakedness in cold weather. But why our translators put Taketh Off into the text passes all effort at comprehension. The original is *adh* with the sign for *out of* in front of it. Altogether it is probable the proverb-maker meant something like this: To sing upon a troubled heart is like vinegar on a wound; or like having one's clothes out of prominence (lost, mislaid, or stolen) in wintry weather.

Just as arrant an impostor as Taketh Off, in the matter of representing *adh*, is Passed On. It is found in the following statement:—

> *Daniel* iii. 27. The satraps, the deputies, and the governors, and the king's counsellors, being gathered together, saw these men that the fire had no power upon their bodies, nor was the hair of their head singed, neither were their hosen changed, nor had the smell of fire *adh* (passed on) them.

But is not this to state something the satraps and others could not have known? That Shadrach and his comrades were not burned, and that neither their hair nor their hosen had suffered they could see; but how could they know that the smell of fire had not *passed on* them? Here again vagueness, or, rather, impossibility, makes us suspect the translation. And what we know of *ad* helps us to correct it. The satraps, having probably sniffed as well as looked, were astonished to find that not only were they not burned, but even the smell of fire was not prominent on them.

Prominence, too, is evidently behind another word chosen by the translators.

> *Job* xl. 10. *Adh* (deck) thyself now with excellency and dignity.

The words seem to say: Thou hast been arraigning God! Make thyself, then, prominent with the eminence, excellence and dignity, proper to God.

Our last example, before turning to the study of Congregation as a rendering of *adh*, is from the prophet Jeremiah:—

Jeremiah xxxi. 4. Again will I build thee, and thou shalt be built, O virgin of Israel: again shalt thou be *adh* (adorned) with thy tabrets, and shalt go forth in the dances of them that make merry.

What is a Tabret? If the reader asks the question of Smith's *Bible Dictionary* he will be referred to Timbrel. Having found Timbrel, he will be shown the picture of an article just like a tambourine. Now let us ask ourselves, Does any virgin, whether of Israel or of the Salvation Army, *adorn* herself with a tambourine? In the case of the latter the answer must be unquestionably, She does not, any more than she adorns herself with her bonnet.

The object of both is not adornment, but that the Salvationist and her endeavours may be made *prominent*. And the promise to Israel is that, returning to Jehovah, she shall once again be prominent with tabrets and in the dance, or that light-hearted gaiety should once more be hers.

CHAPTER IV.

AD AS CONGREGATION.

That was excellently observed, say I, when I read a passage in an author where his opinion agrees with mine. Where we differ, there I pronounce him to be mistaken.—SWIFT.

THE compilers of the Authorised Version were very fond of the word Congregation. Perhaps it was because most of them were preachers. Whatever the reason may have been, they printed it as the representative of three or four Hebrew words, in addition to the several forms of the term whose true meaning we are trying to learn. Among the latter we have already had occasion to mention *moad*, and at this stage it is necessary to look at it again.

The A. V. calls the Tent which stood in the midst of the Israelites' camp the Tabernacle of the Congregation. The revisers were evidently not satisfied with this, and in every case they have replaced it by the Tent of Meeting. In doing so they were probably influenced by such a statement as this: And there I will meet with the children of Israel. The Hebrew, however, is simply Tent *moad*. That is the Prominent Tent, originated and supported by authority. And we have but to think of its position and purpose, its contents, and the Pillar of Cloud resting on its ridge, to see how the name coincides with and confirms what we have found elsewhere.

Here is another text in which *moad* is made to spell Congregation, and with the most bewildering result:—

Psalm lxxv. 2. When I shall receive the congregation I will judge uprightly.

Instead of this the R. V. gives us, When I shall find the set time I will judge uprightly. But something more than the "set time" is needed for righteous judgement. The eminence given by authority and supported by fitness is the great essential. And this is just what *moad* speaks of, or would do if the translators allowed it.

In a psalm immediately preceding that just quoted from *moad* is treated worse than ever:—

Psalm lxxiv. 8. They have burned up all the congregations of God in the land.

The revisers say Synagogues, and very likely among the Appointed Prominences of God here made mention of Synagogues were included. But these were not all. As the context tells us, among the vanished Divine Prominences were Signs, and Prophets, and "Men who know how long."

But, leaving *moad*, *adh* is the form most commonly behind the English word Congregation. In the endeavour to discover its real drift I must advise the reader we are going to venture into a most intricate and perplexing labyrinth. We are not without a clue; but we shall have to walk with careful scrutiny and self-restraint, or we may incur the penalty pronounced by Scripture upon him who breaketh through a hedge.

When we were children, fascinated by the wonderful story of the journeyings of the children of Israel, we were at times not a little puzzled by statements made there about the whole Congregation. The Jewish people on their travels were an immense multitude; not less than six hundred thousand fighting men, besides women and children and Levites. Yet we find the historian speaking like this:—

Exodus xxxv. 20. All the Congregation of Israel departed from the presence of Moses.

Lev. viii. 3. Gather thou all the Congregation together unto the door of the Tabernacle.

Now in trying to estimate the vastness of the demand thus apparently made upon our credulity, we need not think of millions nor of hundreds of thousands. Can we imagine one thousand men gathered at a tent door, or going out from the presence of Moses? But the narrative says again and again, The whole Congregation. Here, once more, is evidently the vague and impossible language that tells of mistranslation.

Of the Manslayer we are told that precautions were to be taken, and cities appointed whither he might flee for refuge, so that he should not be overtaken by vengeance:—

Num. xxxv. 12. Until he stand before the Congregation for judgment.

Can we possibly think that the Manslayer was to stand before, and be tried by, the whole body of the people? Further, it is a direction of the Mosaic Code:—

Lev. xxiv. 16. He that blasphemeth the name of Jehovah, he shall surely be put to death; all the Congregation shall certainly stone him.

AD AS CONGREGATION.

As we read we find ourselves saying involuntarily, But this is not possible! All the Congregation—the women and children included? Or, if only the men are meant, how are they in their hundreds of thousands to get at the culprit, so that "all the Congregation" may have a share in carrying out the sentence?

Common sense alone would assure us that *adh* in these cases cannot mean Congregation. But it is not an easy thing to say off-hand what it does mean. Sometimes there is no difficulty in seeing its purport; as, for instance, in the following verse:—

1 *Kings* viii. 5. And King Solomon and all the Congregation of Israel, that were assembled with him, were with him before the Ark.

Here a reference to the beginning of the chapter from which these words are quoted tells us that this particular "whole congregation" of Israel consisted of the Elders, the Heads of the tribes, and the Princes of fathers' houses. Thus the idea intended to be conveyed by *adh*, and hidden by Congregation, is that of chief, or Prominent, men called together by the king. But if Congregation in this illustration means the nobilities of Israel, what does it signify in the texts that follow?

Num. xx. 2. And there was no water for the *adh* (congregation).

Num. i. 2. Take ye the sum of all the *adh* (congregation) of the children of Israel.

Are we to suppose, in the one case, that it was only the leading men who were thirsty; and, in the other, that these prominent ones numbered, when the sum was taken, not less than six hundred thousand?

The clue to the labyrinth, out of which just here there seems to be no escape except by violence, is in the particular shade of meaning given to our word by the final letter. It looks like a sign of definiteness. We may say it answers the question, What Prominence? by replying, Just that to be expected in the circumstances. We may recur for illustration to the proverb about vinegar on a sore and clothes out of prominence. If we ask what sort of prominence is proper to clothes in wintry weather, the answer will of course be, covering and comforting prominence; no other suits the circumstances.

So the *adh* for whom there was no water must be the definite Prominence suggested by the occasion. What that is may be difficult to decide, for the story is somewhat obscure. It may have been the leaders, or perhaps men appointed to search for water. Only one thing appears to be certain. *Adh* is not identical with the Children of Israel, nor with the Assembly, both of which expressions are found in the context, and to call it Congregation must be erroneous here as elsewhere.

When we turn to other texts there is no difficulty. If we ask what was the *adh* contemplated in the enumeration of the "whole congregation," the answer is plain. The people to be numbered were all males from twenty years old and upward—those that were able to go forth to war in Israel. Thus the particular Prominence pointed to is really the military efficiency of Israel. So our definition of *adh*, as that Prominence proper to the situation, tells us the Manslayer was to appear before the Judicial, and the Blasphemer put to death by the Punitive Prominence appointed for such doings.

No one will expect that all the instances of the use of Congregation, as a substitute for *adh*, in connection with the history of the journeys of Israel can be noticed here. One or two matters of interest may, however, be mentioned.

"Cut off from the Congregation" sounds to some of us a very dreadful doom; and indeed it has been instanced as an example of the "savage ferocity" of the Mosaic Code that a man should be put to death for so trifling a fault as eating leavened bread at Passover time. But this, like so much else, has been forced into the Bible. To "cut a man off" did not mean to kill him; not even when it is declared, That soul shall be cut off from his people. It simply meant Exclusion. For refusing to eat the Passover, and thus to commemorate the redemption of Israel, he was adjudged unworthy to be counted as an Israelite. If "unclean," he was "cut off" from the Assembly. And for eating leavened bread he was not dealt with more severely than the circumstances warranted. He was excluded from any place among the Prominent ones of Israel. Guilty of disobedience himself, it was not thought fitting for him to be a leader of others.

Some of the incidents of the desert journey become much more comprehensible when we read them with the true import of *adh* to guide us. One of these is the account of what took place after the return of the spies from searching the land of Canaan. The explorers told their story, not to the "whole congregation," which would have been impossible, but to Moses and Aaron, and to the *adh* of the children of Israel. Hearing it, the *adh* lifted up their voice and cried; and as the result of such action on the part of the prominent men the people wept, and all the children of Israel murmured. Before the assembly of the *adh* Moses and Aaron fell on their faces. With them Joshua and Caleb expostulated; and it was the *adh* who would have stoned the faithful spies. Then not to the *adh* only, but to all the children of Israel the Glory of Jehovah appeared. Later on the *adh* are spoken of as an evil *adh*, and are doomed to perish in the wilderness.

Another story in which *adh* fills an important part is that of the rebellion of Korah. With him were two hundred and fifty princes of the *adh* called to the *moad*. That is, they were of those whose prominent position in Israel sprung from authority. In a word, they were Levites. They took it into their heads to be jealous of Aaron, and to claim a share in the Priesthood. According to them all the prominent persons in question, not "all the congregation," were holy. In deciding the point, Korah and all his *adh* were to take censers and appear before the Lord. Meanwhile they were reminded by Moses that God had not done a small thing for them in separating them from the ordinary *adh* of Israel before whom they were to stand, and unto whom they were to minister. On the morrow Korah assembled his *adh* unto the door of the Tent of Meeting. Leaving them there for a time, the scene changes to the tents of Korah, Dathan, and Abiram. To the *adh* gathered there Moses cries, Depart! When they are gone the tents sink into the earth. At the other tent, the Tent *moad*, fire comes forth and devours the two hundred that offer incense. The censers used by them were beaten out for a covering for the altar, to be a memorial unto the children of Israel, to the end that no stranger, which is not

AD AS CONGREGATION.   47

of the seed of Aaron, come near to burn incense before the Lord: that he be not as Korah and as his *adh*.

If this should be thought tame and uninteresting no such complaint will be made about the next example. It may be remembered how in the days when Israel was settled in Canaan one of their rulers was famed for feats of strength. When a lion roared against him Samson rent him, as the lion himself might have rent a kid. Passing through the neighbourhood some time after this exploit he went to see if the carcase of the lion were still there. And we read :—

Judges xiv. 8. Behold there was *adh* (a swarm) of bees in the body of the lion, and honey.

This is a unique rendering of *adh*, and, let it be said, a comical. Why did not the translators use the same word so common in other places, and about other things, and write, A Congregation of Bees. The LXX were consistent. They define the *adh* of Israel as the Synagogue of Israel; and when they come to the ribs of the dead lion they tell us there was a synagogue of bees in it. This, too, is funny. But the true absurdity of our English translation is the fact that if it had been literally a *swarm* of bees in the carcase there would have been no honey. Or if by some strange chance there had been, the strength of Samson, like that of the unfortunate bear whose adventures amused us in our nursery days, would not have availed him against a multitude of infuriated bees. What, no doubt, he really saw was the bee-prominence natural to the occasion—laden bees going in with honey, and others coming out in search of more. And undeterred by these occasional and preoccupied busy ones, he could possess himself of the spoil.

But Swarm would do just as well as Congregation in the two texts that follow, for anything either word is able to tell us:—

Job xv. 34. The *adh* (congregation) of hypocrites shall be barren.

Psalm i. 5. The wicked shall not stand in the judgment; nor sinners in the *adh* (congregation) of the righteous.

The verse from Job, taken as it stands, would set us wondering if hypocrites are any more barren than others. As to that, no opinion would be ventured here. But it is suggested the speaker of the words, Eliphaz the Temanite, mistaken as he was in many things, was undoubtedly right in saying the prominence peculiar to hypocrisy must eventually prove fruitless as regards anything of worth.

And the writer of the first psalm was too shrewd a man to say sinners shall not stand in or enter the congregation of the righteous. He, like chanters of his psalm in sacred places to-day, must have had misgivings about that. But he could see, and sing, the impossibility of sinners attaining to the *adh* of the righteous; that is, to the peculiar eminence belonging only to goodness.

One more quotation, and then we may proceed to the final and most important stage of our inquiry as to the significance of *ad*.

Psalm lxxxii. 1. God standeth in the *adh* (congregation) of the Mighty.
He judgeth among the gods.

The reader will perhaps be surprised to learn that God and Mighty in this verse represent the same Hebrew word, and had the translators been consistent they would have rendered, God standeth in the congregation of God. The revisers have done so. But of all the instances of the unsuitability of Congregation to set forth the meaning of *adh* none is more conclusive than this. The context shows the idea of the psalmist to be, that God is standing among other gods to "judge" them—to put them right by counsel and rebuke; and to speak of this concourse of "gods" as the Congregation of God is to miss the mark. When the Almighty is represented as saying to Job, Since thou arraignest Jehovah, deck thyself with honour and majesty, the sense is that Job is given to understand he must be able to assume the greatness proper to God before he can be in a position to accuse Him. And this is the force of *adh* in the passage before us. Among the gods, to threaten and advise, the Most High stands in that might and majesty which qualify Him to be their Judge—God standeth in the Prominence of God.

CHAPTER V.

AD AS "WITNESS."

The world owes all its onward impulses to men ill at ease. The happy man inevitably confines himself within ancient limits.
· HAWTHORNE.

THE thoughtful reader of the New Testament has probably taken note of the fact that the word Witness is one of the most familiar and weighty words to be found in its pages. He will recall it in such sayings as, To this end am I come into the world, that I should bear witness unto the truth; Ye shall be witnesses unto Me; Seeing we are compassed about with so great a cloud of witnesses; and, The faithful and true witness, viz., Jesus Christ. But perhaps he is not aware that these and other uses of the word in the New Testament cannot be understood in all their fulness of meaning and allusion without a knowledge of the Hebrew *ad*. And this is only another way of saying that Witness is not able to give a complete account of what was in the writer's mind, whether he wrote in the Old Testament or in the New.

This will be seen if we ponder such a text as :—

Exodus xx. 16. Thou shalt not bear false witness against thy neighbour.

This commandment, like the others, is exceeding broad; but the use of the word Witness has a tendency, in many minds, to narrow it until it means little more than speaking truth in the witness-box, or, perhaps, abstinence from slander and scandal. Much more, however, is required. It forbids the raising of false prominences of every kind; of flattery and adulation, no less than those of calumny and detraction. And further, it guards against raising false hopes, unwarranted faith, unreal content, or any kind of lying prominence *in* our neighbour.

If what I write has the appearance of finding fault with other men's work, the reader is entreated to believe that this is not the motive. Not a word more of the kind is said than is essential to the purpose in hand, and that is the restoration and confirmation of the true meaning of Biblical words. In translating *ad* by Witness, the A.V. sometimes employs the best word in our language; sometimes it does not. But whatever the rendering chosen, it is contended here that in every passage where Witness occurs as representative of *ad* the Hebrew word is used to speak either of Prominence in itself, or to give prominence to something else. And this distinction should be borne in mind. A witness is not necessarily a prominent person in himself; he stands in the box to give prominence to certain facts. When this is *ad's* work, when it simply has to make something evident or conspicuous, Witness is a good equivalent. But when *ad* appears to stand for Prominence directly, or for something as being prominent in itself, then Witness does not seem competent to do the work for which it has been selected. Keeping this in view, let us turn to the instances.

Exodus xxii. 12, 13. If it be stolen from him he shall make restitution unto the owner thereof. If it be torn in pieces let him bring it for *ad* (witness); he shall not make good that which is torn.

This regulation tells us the man to whom an animal was delivered to "keep" was responsible for the depredations of human robbers, but not for loss occasioned by four-legged marauders. If he alleged the latter cause, he was to bring the torn carcase for witness. No better word can be found, probably, than Witness to express the idea. Still it cannot but be seen that the torn carcase is brought in to give convincing prominence to the fact asserted.

So it is when *ad* is used by Bible writers to speak of the Witnesses to a marriage. The union of Boaz and Ruth is a case in point. We read that at the gate of the city, where matters of important business were commonly settled, Boaz took his seat, together with ten Elders and a near kinsman of Naomi's husband and sons. This near kinsman had the first claim on the hand of Ruth, but declined to exercise it. To show this, according to custom, he took off his shoe and, just as though Ruth were in it, handed it to Boaz. This the narrator says was for *ad*, or, as our version has it, for Testimony; it made the relinquishment of his right publicly prominent. Upon this Boaz said to the Elders and to the people :—

Ruth iv. 9-11. Ye are Witnesses this day that I have bought all that was Elimelech's, and all that was Chilion's and Mahlon's, of the hand of Naomi. Moreover Ruth the Moabitess, the wife of Mahlon, have I purchased to be my wife. . . . Ye are witnesses this day. And all the people that were in the gate and the Elders, said, We are Witnesses.

Here again the use of the English word is happy. If the marriage of Boaz should at any time be out of prominence (like the garment in wintry weather), if doubt should be thrown upon its having taken place, these Elders, and others, were in a position to give it prominence in men's knowledge and belief.

On the other hand there are texts where, as already intimated, Witness is out of place, and its presence misleading. But here, also, the original thought seems clearly to support us in the opinion we have taken up as to *ad's* intention.

Micah i. 2. Hear, ye peoples, all of you; hearken, O earth, and all that therein is: and let the Lord God be witness against you, the Lord from His holy temple.

The revisers in their margin suggest that the word "against" in this text should be changed to *among*, but they go no further than the margin. The thought of the A.V. seems to have been that *ad* must mean Witness, and that Jehovah in such a relation could only be a witness *against* men. And this thought they have allowed to govern them in many places, to the detriment of exact truth. That God, or a prophet, must necessarily be a witness antagonistic to men arises from a kind of exaggeration in religion, already spoken of, which has been a great hindrance to correct interpretation. In the text before us the sense is, Let the Lord God be prominent with you.

It is as though Micah said, Think of Him; picture Him to yourselves; give unto Him the weight due to His name.

In a quotation from another prophet :—

Malachi iii. 5. And I will come near you to judgment; and I will be a swift Witness against the sorcerers, and against the adulterers, and against false swearers, and against those that oppress the hireling in his wages, the widow, and the fatherless, and that turn aside the stranger, and fear not Me, saith the Lord.

We may perhaps allow "against" to stand; at all events, there is not the same objection to its presence. But it is evident the prophet, when he speaks of Jehovah as being a swift Prominence, means much more than Witness. He can hardly imply less than that Jehovah will be Witness, Judge, and Executioner all in one.

A more familiar text is:—

Isaiah lv. 4. Behold I have given him for a witness to the peoples, a leader and commander to the peoples.

The taking of witness here in a rigidly literal sense has led to the saying of many things, some of them quite astonishing. David did testify by his reign and victories to his possession of kingly and military qualities; generally, too, he was a witness for Righteousness, and gave Prominence to God. But probably Isaiah, in the words before us, simply intends to say that David was given as a prominent prince and leader.

Job, in his trouble, is made by our version to say:—

Job x. 17. Thou renewest Thy witnesses against me,
And increasest Thine indignation upon me;
Changes and warfare are with me.

But if there was one thing more than another the absence of which Job in his complaint against God comments upon, it is that of evidence. Again and again does he ask for witness to the truth of his friends' assertion that his affliction is a punishment; and for witness to contradict his own declaration of innocence. And to make him say to God, Thou renewest Thy witnesses against me, is to obscure the text and contradict the context. What he does declare is rather that God has multiplied prominent sorrows and pains, so that host after host is against him.

In another quotation from Job our English Bible reads:—

Job xxix. 11, 12. For when the ear heard me, then it blessed me;
And when the eye saw me, it gave witness to me:
Because I delivered the poor that cried,
The fatherless also, that had none to help him.

Not so much exception can be taken to the choice of witness in this instance. But it may further our object if we ask how an eye can give witness in such a case as Job is speaking of. Not by weeping, nor by winking. The eye can, and does, "bear witness" at times in those ways, but here it can only do so by admiration. In other words, the eye makes Job a prominent object in its regard.

Returning for a moment to the arbitrary insertion of the word Against, as causing ambiguity, there is an interesting example in what an historian appears to say about Samuel, or represents Samuel as saying about himself, which becomes more lucid in the light of our theory:—

1 *Sam.* xii. 3. Here I am: witness against me before the Lord, and before His anointed: whose ox have I taken? or whose ass have I taken? or whom have I defrauded?

In this verse Witness does not stand for *ad*, but for another word, which means Answer. The people having answered that he had not defrauded them, Samuel goes on to say:—

Verse 5. The Lord is witness against you, and His anointed is witness this day, that ye have not found aught in my hand. And they said, He is witness.

This time *ad* is the word represented by Witness, both in the declaration of Samuel and in the rejoinder of the people. But see what a mess the obtrusion of Against makes of things. It gives us the impression that the people have been accusing Samuel of fraud, and that he points to the Lord and His anointed as witnessing against them to the contrary. But the people have, only just before, averred their belief in his integrity. And what Samuel really says is the opposite of Against you. He claims that God and His anointed are witnesses with them, *i.e.* on the same side, in evidencing his uprightness. The argument is something like this: If I were unworthy of the office I am now relinquishing I should not to-day be in the enjoyment of God's favour and the king's. The fact that I have not forfeited either is proof that both God and the king make the fact of my righteousness prominent. Is it not so? And all the people answered (in the one word *ad*), Prominent.

At the risk of being wearisome something must be said, before closing the first part of our inquiry, about what I may call the monumental *ads* of Scripture; for these, more than any other, have influenced the New Testament writers in their use of the word Witness; and from them, too, comes the strongest corroboration of our opinion. In a way they are something like our milestones, giving prominence to distance, and the gravestones, which, however humble and worthless in themselves, afford prominence to something about somebody who has died.

To recall one of our illustrations, these modern stone *ads*, like those of which we are about to think, fill the purpose of a ☞, directing attention to something thought worthy of notice.

The first of these to come under our eyes is that mentioned in the account of the parting between Laban and Jacob:—

Gen. xxxi. 51, 52. And Laban said to Jacob, Behold this heap, and behold this pillar, which I have set betwixt me and thee. This heap be witness, and this pillar be witness, that I will not pass over this heap to thee, and that thou shalt not pass over this heap and this pillar unto me for harm.

Before investigating these words there is an amusing instance of the misuse of *ad* in an earlier part of the story, which ought not to be passed by without notice. It is in the verse:—

Gen. xxxi. 24. The God of your fathers spake unto me yesternight, saying, Take heed to thyself that thou speak not to Jacob *ad* (either) good or bad.

If a man is to speak neither good nor bad, what *is* he to say? We might expect to find a dumb interview following the words, or, at most, a hesitating speech about some indifferent topic. As a matter of fact, we find Laban talking away without any difficulty, and soundly rating Jacob for having stolen his gods. The command, however, to Laban, when we read it rightly, was not to speak to Jacob "*ad* from good to bad." He had just cause to complain; but out of that "good" he was not to make evil prominent. The order was obeyed, and nothing worse than mutual accusation followed.

To return to the monuments. The heap and pillar were set up for "Witness" to a covenant made between them. The agreement was that neither should pass beyond the pillar and the heap on the way to each other "for harm." Thus the erections were *ad*. There was no inscription on them; the ordinary wayfarer would learn nothing from them. But if in the future there should be cause for anger, and one should be in danger of invading the other, the silent witness would remind Laban and Jacob of the solemn circumstances in which they had agreed not to pass it for harm, and so it would give prominence to their covenant.

As Laban and Jacob spoke different, yet kindred, languages they did not call the monument by the same name. To Laban it was *Jegar-sahadutha*; to Jacob *Galad*. If the reader looks closely he will find *ad* in both names. The words occur again in the Book of Job, though, judging from the English Version, no one would think so.

Job xvi. 18, 19. O earth, cover not thou my blood,
And let my cry have no place.
And now, behold, my witness is in heaven,
And my record is on high.

Jacob's word is behind witness in the third line, and Laban's is turned into record, or, in the R.V., he that voucheth for me. But to read like this is to put the text out of harmony with the context. Job is complaining that God is against him. God has set him up as a mark to shoot at; has run upon him like a giant. How can he in the same breath speak of God as He who voucheth for me? It seems clear that, to say nothing of the other word, *ad* in this place is not properly represented by

Witness; that is to say, it is not used in Job's speech to make something prominent, but to speak of something already prominent in itself. And the drift of the quotation is probably something like this: The earth cannot cover my blood, and my cry cannot be hushed; for the prominence of my trouble is in the heavens, and its memorial in the heights.

Returning for a moment to the story in Genesis, the reader will see a resemblance between Jacob's word, Galeed, and the name of a country, Gilead. Stripped of the vowel-points the words are identical. The first part of the word, *gl*, means heap, and is used in the Bible to speak of the waves of the sea. From this we might be led to imagine Gilead was so called because people thought its heights resembled petrified wave-like prominences. So that Gilead is literally Wave-Prominence. Wave-Witness, it may be said, would be wrong, because the hills to which allusion is made are not like a ☞, but are prominent in themselves. According to travellers, Gilead is just what its name, reading *ad* as we have done, would lead us to expect. Dean Stanley speaks of it as a high table-land tossed into wild confusion of undulating downs.

But we must pass on to notice some other monumental prominences. One of these is mentioned in the following verses :—

Joshua xxiv. 26, 27. He took a great stone and set it up there under the oak that was by the sanctuary of the Lord. And Joshua said unto all the people, Behold this stone shall be a witness against us; for it hath heard all the words of the Lord, which He spake unto us; it shall be therefore a witness against you, lest ye deny your God.

The wording of the last clause is not worthy. How could witnessing *against* be a prevention of apostacy? The sense of course is: This stone shall be a reminder to you of Jehovah's goodness, lest ye deny your God. And there is a thought behind the erection of this monument which deserves to be called into prominence. A little while before we read :—

Joshua xxiv. 21, 22. The people said unto Joshua, Nay, but we will serve the Lord. And Joshua said unto the people, Ye are witnesses with yourselves that ye have chosen you the Lord to serve Him. And they said, We are witnesses.

They themselves, by their voices, gave prominence to the resolve to serve God. But we know how much that is worth. The vow was speedily and frequently broken; and Joshua knew that the best safeguard against apostacy and the strongest inducement to return is something that will make prominent the Divine Goodness. The people were themselves that also; they were, as we say, monuments of mercy. Their eyes had seen the cloudy pillar, their ear had hearkened to the voice of the fire, their mouths had eaten manna, they had drunk of the rock that followed them. What need had they of further memorial? But, as we know, eyes and ears, and mouths and hands, have other and very different memories beside those connected with the love of God. And Joshua illustrated and filled a need of human nature when, choosing a monument with no other story to tell, he set it up as an everlasting, unchanging ☞ pointing to Jehovah's mercy, lest they should deny their God.

What Joshua did in a comparatively small way Moses

did in a greater. Shortly before his death he is reported as saying :—

Deut. xxxi. 28. Assemble unto me all the elders of your tribes, and your officers, that I may speak these words in their ears, and call heaven and earth to witness against you.

The expression suggesting antagonisn is once more an intruder. So is the word Call. The idea seems to be, I will fill the heavens and the earth with memorials and reminders. It is as though one were to say, The heavens and the earth are prominent in themselves and in their contents, I will make them prominent in another way; they shall point to lessons that make for righteousness. The words are spoken of his Song, which was in itself to be preserved as a "witness." If we turn to the Song, we see at a glance that "heaven and earth" are indeed made to speak. Rain and dew, grass and herb, rock and eagle, oil and honey, burning heat and fire, the fangs of beasts and the poison of serpents, are pressed into the service, until everywhere there are pointers indicating the worth of right and the evil of wrong as viewed by the prophet of Jehovah.

But as we look back on all the life-history of Moses, and especially if we pierce the veil of the miraculous and recognize the lessons of Egypt and the Sea, of the Manna and the Rock, the Divine Fire and the trackless desert journey, as they were recognized by the Hebrew seers, we shall take up his own words and apply them to his whole work and say, He filled the heavens and the earth with signs that give prominence to Jehovah and His dealings with men.

The most potent "witness" this high bard and great old saint of other days gave to his people was the writing on the Tables of the Ten Words. This was the great *ad*, or, let us say, Prominentor, of Old Testament days. And that fact is recognized in the language of Israel. Tabernacle and Veil and Ark are all called by its name. After three thousand years it still points its stony finger, immovable and undecaying, to the regions of God and duty; and the whole experience of men is the proof that it does not err. One greater than Moses has said it will not fail till all be accomplished.

Greater and yet like unto Moses. And after our search in Old Testament pages it is an advantage to us to find we can turn to the New and read with clearer knowledge, and see our final illustration of *ad* in Jesus Christ. For He is called the faithful and true ☞. To this end was He born, that He might give prominence to the truth; or, and better, to what is real. And there are those who think they see in this fact the "promise and potency" of a universal kingdom. Meanwhile His followers, by word and life, are to be His "witnesses," His indicators. And, to cheer them on, they are encompassed about with a great cloud of witnesses, all pointing to the certain victory of faith.

CHAPTER VI.

OLAM.

The Hebrew Bible, is it not, before all things, true, as no other book ever was or will be?—CARLYLE.

THERE has been a hidden motive behind our long pursuit of *ad* in its various forms and numerous appearances which must come to light if only for a moment.

The opinion that *olam* is a Time and Eternity word is so ancient, so rooted, and so almost universally prevalent, that it was feared some readers would not consent even to consider the possibility of its being erroneous without the stimulus of some preparatory encouragement. If *ad*, another word taken to have the same meaning and almost as authoritatively, were first exhaustively treated, if its real significance could be conclusively set forth, then perhaps the timid, and especially those in bondage to preconception, might be induced to proceed, asking themselves the question, If a mistake has been made as to one word, said to mean For ever, why might it not be so with another? Having said so much, and knowing what is to follow, I will venture to predict that the evidence for the true sense of *olam*, if it can be faithfully presented and viewed with unveiled face, will be felt to be, if possible, more abundant, more striking, and more conclusive than that which has accumulated in our investigation of *ad*.

Olam is one of the greatest of words. It embodies a conception which in many of its applications is among the sublimest things even in Scripture. It helps us to realize what a great thing revelation is. Moreover, it has the advantage of being open to proof, a quality, as previously observed, not possessed by For ever and ever.

It is used by the Bible writers to qualify God, sun, moon, and earth, deserts, peoples, priesthoods, landmarks, slavery, Canaan, paths, mountains, doors, statutes, and thrones. *Olam* Embracing, *olam* Joy, Love, and Peace, and *olam* Strength, Confusion, and Reproach, are also frequent Biblical expressions.

The examples in the last sentence and many of the others come before us in our version in some such form as Everlasting, Perpetual, or For ever. In almost every instance the idea of Duration, either brief or endless, is suggested. And this is representative of that ancient and deep-rooted opinion to which reference has been made. Dr. Plumptre in his commentary on Ecclesiastes (one of the best of a valuable series of volumes) says roundly: No other meaning but that of a duration, the end or beginning of which is hidden from us, and which, therefore, is infinite, or, at least, indefinite, is ever connected with it in the Hebrew of the Old Testament. This from such a source is enough to give us pause. And behind it are the Fathers, most of them, the Churches, the Theologies, and, with a few exceptions, the Commentators, not to mention Lexicons. Every reader should know this; although, knowing it, the effect should be to make him think it altogether impossible that the question can be reopened. I, even now as I write, can hardly help thinking it impossible myself.

Let us, however, examine a statement similar to that made by Dr. Plumptre, and taken from a learned volume whose title I cannot just now bring to mind :—

"The root of *olam* means to *hide*. From this root-meaning arose the conception of *hidden time*, that is to say, of duration, the beginning or the ending of which is hidden from us. From this again came the idea of eternity."

Now here and in the words of Dr. Plumptre we have a sample of a habit of writing into which men have allowed themselves to fall in dealing with the Bible. "The root-meaning of *olam* is to *hide*." "No other meaning but that of a duration, the end or beginning of which is hidden from us, and which therefore is infinite, or at least indefinite, is ever connected with it in the Hebrew of the Old Testament." Men are not permitted to treat of frogs and spiders in that way. There they must give reasons, and not only that, they must lay bare the course of observation which led them to their conclusions. It has been said, The exclusive test of knowledge of a subject is the power to teach it. But to say the root-meaning of *olam* is to *hide*, that from this root there sprouted the idea of Hidden Duration, and from this again the further idea of Eternity, is not to teach us anything. If the power to teach be behind the statement it is kept out of sight. When a man of science offers a conjecture about the frog or the spider he is listened to with respect. So it should be with the conjectures of Biblical scholars. But dogmatic assertions, except as the outcome of demonstration, should have less weight in their case, because of the importance of the subject, than they have in the case of the scientist.

But let us put this hidden-time significance imposed upon *olam* to the test of investigation.

> *Ps.* xc. 8. Thou hast set our iniquities before Thee;
> Our *olams* (secret sins) in the light of Thy countenance

The translators have not turned *olam* into hidden time, or short or long duration, but into Secret Sins; so that, if it were worth while, we might claim them as allies. But we should soon have to part from them again. In this text there is nothing about sins in the Hebrew; the insertion of the word in the English is another instance of unconscious religious exaggeration. The passage reads, Thou hast set . . . our *olams* in the light of Thy countenance. What are our *olams*? Well, if we accept the "root-meaning," and the sproutings from it, we must say, Thou hast set our Hidden Durations, or our Eternities, in the light of Thy countenance. Perhaps the reader feels informed and satisfied with that? If he is, let him proceed to read a somewhat similar passage in the same way :—

> *Eccles.* iii. 11. He hath made everything beautiful in His time : also He hath set *olam* (A.V. the World, R.V. Eternity) in their heart, so that no man can find out the work that God maketh from the beginning to the end.

The idea embodied in these words seems to be: The reason why men do not see that everything God has made is beautiful is that they do not understand God's work from beginning to end; and the reason they do not understand is because He hath set *olam* in their heart. But what *olam* means here, and how it acts as a restraint to knowledge, the translators and revisers, and the other scholars mentioned, do not tell us—at least, not with unanimity. "The word," they appear to say, "is a fearsome word for perplexing people, especially in this place. Some of us think it means, God hath set the world in man's heart; others think the writer would have us believe God hath put Eternity there; the rest of us would say it is Duration, the beginning or the end of which is hidden, that is in question. You, O reader, must take your choice from what we offer you, and make the best of it." And the reader will probably think it the most astounding choice ever offered him on any subject.

But, keeping this so-called root-meaning before us, let us turn to an exclamation often met with in the historical parts of the Bible—O king, live for ever! Our English shout, Long live the Queen! we may say Amen to; we understand its meaning. But did anybody, even in an Eastern court, ever say, O king, may you never die? for that is, of course, the literal meaning of O King, live for ever. Be that as it may, we shall be quite sure no one so much as thought of saying, O king, live for duration— the beginning or end of which is hidden from us, and which is therefore infinite, or at least indefinite. But some critics will be for calling this puerile, though they might safely be challenged to point out any difference in absurdity between the phrase as given in the English Bible and the variation of it just suggested.

Hid, or Hidden, does sometimes give a very good account of the drift of *olam*; but whether in such cases it bears out the Hidden Time theory or not the reader will judge. Here are some examples:—

Lev. iv. 13. And if the whole congregation of Israel shall err, and the thing be *olam* (hid) from the eyes of the Assembly.

2 *Chron.* ix. 2. There was nothing *olam* (hid) from Solomon which he told her not.

Job xxviii. 20, 21. Whence then cometh wisdom?
And where is the place of understanding?
Seeing it is *olam* (hid) from the eyes of all living.

As was said, the translators' word Hid is a good equivalent for *olam* in these texts. But the assertion we have in mind declares no other meaning but that of a duration the end or beginning of which is hidden from us is ever connected with *olam* in the Hebrew of the Old Testament. Where, then, is the idea of Hidden Time in the passages just quoted? The reader can search for it; and, not finding it, he will say the assertion, given without evidence, is disproved.

Leaving this theory behind, we may ask as we proceed, Is the idea of something hidden that general meaning of *olam* which, according to our rules, we should expect it to have everywhere? The answer to the question is, No, or we should have to read Isaiah as telling us:—

Isaiah xxxv. 10. And *olam* (hidden) joy shall be upon their heads.

Isaiah lx. 19. Jehovah shall be thine *olam* (hidden) light.

This would never do; therefore Hidden cannot be the general meaning of *olam*. And as a matter of fact we shall find that in the passages where Hid serves so well it is not the primary meaning of *olam*, but only one of its results.

In the texts just given from Isaiah the word used by the translators is Everlasting. Here, again, we may come to see that never-ending duration may be predicted of a thing as a consequence of its being *olam*, but neither in these cases nor elsewhere is it the first and great meaning; and to this point the battle has now to be turned. In doing so, let it be borne in mind that, so far as I can learn, nobody has ever set forth any kind of proof that *olam* does mean Everlasting. Almost everybody says it does, but that is another thing. If we go to the lexicon, the lexicon sends us to the translation; if we ask the scholar, he points us to the dictionary. If we ask for proof of the conclusions there, or for a path by which we may reach them for ourselves, people appear not to understand. Yet in the interests of truth and religion this question as to the exact meaning of *olam* is one of great moment.

In our inquiry we will proceed as before, putting *olam* into the text of the quotations, and setting the English word chosen by the translators to represent it in brackets. If the reader will accustom himself to read *olam* instead of the English word, I think he will find that it will gradually translate itself to him.

We will begin with citations in which no one will say that *olam* suggests the idea of Eternity.

Proverbs xxii. 28. Remove not the *olam* (ancient) landmark which thy fathers have set.

Isaiah lxi. 4. And they shall build the *olam* (old) wastes.

Isaiah xlii. 14. I have *olam* (long time) holden my peace.

Psalm cxliii. 3. He hath smitten me down to the ground:
He hath made me to dwell in dark places
As those who have been *olam* (long) dead.

If *olam* does in any case imply Eternity, and if there be truth in our theory, then in these instances we should have to read of an Everlasting landmark, and of building, or restoring, never-ending ruins; we should hear Jehovah, or His prophet, speaking of eternal silence in the past, and the psalmist alluding to people who had been eternally dead! But it will, of course, be objected by people who have not accepted our creed that although *olam* in these texts cannot be intended to convey the idea of perpetuity, this is no reason why it should not do so in others.

Let us turn, then, to instances of the use of *olam* in which the translators have put For ever, and that, so far as may be seen, without the slightest hesitation, and certainly without a suggested alternative. The first in our list will be found sufficiently amusing:—

Isaiah xxxii. 14, 15. The populous city shall be deserted; the hill and the watch-tower shall be dens *olam* (*for ever*), a joy of wild asses, a pasture of flocks; until the spirit be poured out from on high, and the wilderness become a fruitful field, and the fruitful field be counted for a forest.

The hill and the watch-tower are to be dens *olam*. This the translators say means dens for ever. But the prophet himself proceeds immediately to contradict them. The hill and the watch-tower are not to be dens for ever, but only until the Spirit be poured out from on high.

The next quotation is of a much graver character, and will bring us into the very thick of the fight:—

Exodus xxxii. 13. Remember Abraham, Isaac, and Israel, Thy servants to whom Thou swarest by Thine own self, and saidst unto them, I will multiply your seed as the stars of heaven, and all this land that I have spoken of will I give unto your seed, and they shall inherit it *olam* (for ever).

If our word is correctly put into English here, what is to be said of the promise? For Canaan is not now, and has not been for many centuries, the inheritance of Israel. A belief in the veracity of Scripture, that when it says For ever it means no less, has led many people to treat this and similar passages in a fashion that has done harm to the cause of religion by excluding the Bible from that position in the estimation of thoughtful persons to which its surpassing worth entitles it. Canaan, it has been said, is not Canaan really, but a type of Heaven; and the children of Abraham are not the Jewish people, but the offspring of Abraham's faith. But in the words quoted Moses is pleading for a set of people who were certainly not the children of Abraham's faithfulness! Will anyone say that he was reminding God of a promise to give them Heaven for ever?

Another explanation tells us the promise of Canaan as an inheritance is only delayed. Its fulfilment will come; Israel will be gathered from the ends of the earth and re-established in the land given to Abraham. Let us suppose this to be so, would the prediction, as we read it in our Bible, be accomplished? Not in the strict sense of the words For ever. Eternity can have no break in it any more than it can have an end.

Another instance of the same difficulty may be given:—

Exodus xl. 15. And thou shalt bring his sons and put coats upon them; and thou shalt anoint them as thou didst anoint their father, that they may minister unto Me in the priest's office: and their anointing shall be to them for an *olam* (everlasting) priesthood throughout their generations.

It may be the Jewish people think their priests will

succeed each other in an everlasting succession, but Christians, not even the translators, despite their choice of a word signifying unending duration, do not take that to be the meaning of the text. Some of the commentators tell us the word in this instance means, Everlasting till its work was done. If so, Everlasting has, literally, no business to appear in such a connection. Others say the priesthood is carried on in Christ. But the main argument of one of the most profound of the New Testament writers is really based upon the fact that our Lord did not spring from the Aaronic priesthood, and had nothing in common with it.

To the same class belong the texts which are made to speak of the perpetual continuance of the throne of David. One instance will suffice:—

> *Psalm* lxxxix. 35-37. Once have I sworn by My holiness;
> I will not lie unto David:
> His seed shall endure *olam* (for ever),
> And his throne as the sun before Me.
> It shall be established *olam* (for ever) as the moon,
> And as the faithful witness in the sky.

It is confidently said the reference here is Messianic. Perhaps in some way it is. Whether or no, I believe the words of the angel Gabriel respecting Jesus, God shall give unto Him the throne of His father David, and He shall reign "unto the ages"; and (a very different matter from the foregoing clause) of His kingdom there shall be no end. But I do not see how I, or any man of ordinary sanity, can believe that the psalmist spoke of David with his lips, but meant Christ in his heart. As little can I accept the argument which says the words must refer to Christ, because if they do not the prediction is not true, it is not fulfilled. For this argument rests upon the idea that *olam* in the mouth of the psalmist meant For ever, and that idea is not true. The psalmist in the verses next following those quoted goes on to say:—

> But Thou hast cast off and rejected,
> Thou hast been wroth with Thine anointed.
> Thou hast abhorred the covenant of Thy servant;
> Thou hast profaned his crown even to the ground.

We must all be getting rather tired of merely adverse criticism, and our examination of these texts about Canaan, the priesthood, and the throne of David is the last blow of the kind to be dealt at the theory of the endless duration-meaning of *olam*. Is any further attack needed? What we have seen leaves us in this dilemma: If *olam* means For ever, the Bible, in the passages noticed, is proved by events to have spoken falsely; if the Bible is true, *olam* does not mean For ever.

Two other instances of *olam's* use will serve to put us on the track of the true import of the word:—

Jonah ii. 6. I went down to the bottoms of the mountains.
    The earth with her bars was about me *olam* (for ever).

Eccles. iii. 14. I know that whatsoever God doeth it shall be *olam* (for ever): nothing can be put to it, nor anything taken from it.

Now, as anybody can see, Jonah could not say the earth-bars were about him for ever; he was not there long enough to know. And the writer of Ecclesiastes could not say, being the wise man he was, that everything God doeth is for ever; facts would contradict him. What did they say?

The later author defines his meaning. According to him *olam* is a fixed thing, unalterable by addition or by subtraction. So, among other things, the moon is *olam;* man can put nothing to it, nor can he take anything from it. And Jonah declares the earth-bars were about him to a certainty; it was a fact, unexaggerated and irreducible. And glancing back for a moment, this is what was really stated about Canaan, the priesthood, and David's throne. They were to be for certain, as we say; they were Fixities, sure to be. But as to how long they were to continue so *olam* has nothing whatever to tell us.

Before I go on to show how this interpretation of *olam* covers the whole ground there is one other case in which it is translated For ever to which I must refer. It is of great interest not only in itself, but from the fact that some of the most strenuous advocates of the accepted translation would, if pressed to extremes, utterly repudiate it in particular instances. On the other hand, the reading of *olam* advocated in these pages would seem to entail the very thought these inconsistent people would thus cast away. I speak of the many times repeated words,

His mercy endureth *olam* (for ever).

The word "endureth" has nothing in the Hebrew to warrant its presence in the text. It has been put in, and it stands there as a cogent witness to the strength of the preconception as to the duration-significance of *olam*. The original is, in colloquial English, simply, His mercy is for certain. Now, as I have intimated, people who would demur to our rendering, and indeed to any alteration of the familiar words, would at the same time refuse to carry out the statement made in the common translation to legitimate conclusions. If asked, Does this saying, in your opinion, really mean that the mercy of God *never* ceases? we know the answer that would be given.

It is said of Napoleon that hearing a painting spoken of as an immortal work he asked how long it would last. "Well," someone, rather at a loss what to say, replied, "perhaps four or five hundred years." "*Belle immortalité!*" exclaimed the Emperor with much disdain. But there are men and women who stand up in our sanctuaries and say or chant, His mercy endureth for ever, who really ascribe to For ever a much briefer life than five hundred years. For threescore years and ten the individual man is, perhaps, sure of mercy, and then the text often quoted is not, His mercy endureth for ever, but, As the tree falls so it will lie.

But, in fact, trees do not lie as or where they fall, they are wanted elsewhere. And if they did so lie, that would have nothing to tell us as to the fate of men. This is altogether an unreality from which we need deliverance. There ought not to be antagonism between our words and our belief, especially in Church. And the true meaning of *olam* does deliver us. The old-time Hebrew in his chant had no thought of time or of eternity. He contented himself with saying, The mercy of Jehovah is a certainty; and he knew that what he thus declared was open to demonstration.

Yet, as we shall see later, it may be argued, if not proved, from the fact of mercy or loving-kindness being a fixture, it is also, and therefore, everlasting.

CHAPTER VII.

OLAM AS FIXITY.

The Bible has not been injured by unbelievers. The obscurities which alone mar its beauty and lessen its power are the results of the well-meant labour of its admirers and friends.

FIXITY, or the old-fashioned Fixation, or the more familiar Fixture, seem to give a good account in English of the general meaning of *olam*. We must, however, remember that they include the ideas of Stability and Certainty. And though we might incline to think it a trivial matter whether *olam* speaks of a thing as stable or as certain, we shall find there are texts where it is of the greatest importance to find an exact definition. But before treating of these shades of meaning we had better inquire what support there may be for our theory so far as stated.

We must not suppose that *olam*, in speaking of a Fixture, says necessarily that a thing does not move or that it cannot change. A Hebrew observer watching the moon saw that it altered its position, that it waxed and waned, that it disappeared from sight. Yet to him the moon was *olam;* he knew it was sure to reappear, and that all its movements and changes were in reality fixtures.

On the other hand, a man returning from long exile would be certain to find one feature of his home unchanged. His house might be overthrown, his neighbours

OLAM AS FIXITY.

might be gone, the trees blown down, the river dried up, but the mountains would be there. So it came to pass that the mountains were thought of and spoken of as *olam*. There are people of whom it is said:—

Psalm xlix. 11. Their inward thought is that their houses shall continue (*olam*) for ever.

But it is not so. The Bible speaks of *olam* tents, but they are not pitched here on earth. Man and his dwelling-place, his glory and his wealth, are never spoken of as *olam*. To the Hebrew seer man is as grass, and human glory as the flower of grass. And to him, while the grass withers, and the flower fades, the word of Jehovah does neither; it is *olam*.

It is interesting to note that the word is never used of the sea. Some of our own poets have told us the sea belongs to eternity, not to time, that time writes no wrinkle on its azure brow. But the Hebrew did not love the sea. He preferred that someone else should do business for him in great waters. The symbolism of ocean did not suggest to him something eternal; his insight told him the time would come when there would be no more sea. But as he stood and watched its raging and listened to its roar, the beach or the rock beneath his feet was emphatically *olam*.

Jer. v. 22. Will ye not tremble at My presence, which have placed the sand for the bound of the sea by an *olam* (perpetual) decree, that it cannot pass it? And though the waves thereof toss themselves, yet can they not prevail; though they roar, yet can they not pass over it.

It would hardly be possible to find a more striking illustration of the true force of *olam* than that afforded by this quotation, or one that admits us to a clearer view of those regions where, on the lips of Hebrew seers, *olam* does its most important work. The waves toss and roar; in awful weight and fury they dash upon the beach. But to-morrow they will be hushed and still. The shore may be strewn with wreckage, but the boundary set by the Creator will not have been overpassed. So, as these prophets would teach us, it is in other scenes, beset with other tempests. There *olam* points, not to the uprising of evil, not to the breaking forth of wrath, and the darkness shrouding the light, but to the decree which saith, Thus far shalt thou come, but no farther.

If we now glance back at some of the instances of the use of *olam* brought forward in the last chapter we shall find fresh confirmation. It will be remembered we objected to the word Hid as an equivalent for the Hebrew, though at the same time it was hinted no exception could be taken to it as a consequent meaning. A thing hidden from the eyes of an assembly is really so hidden because it is fixed from their knowledge. So, in the thought of Job, Wisdom is fixed from the eyes of all living. No one will suppose that any fault is found with the translation in these cases as being insufficient to give the sense of the original; they are simply recalled to show that even where the rendering is satisfactory the thought of *olam* is still that of Fixity. When we, any of us, try to conceal a thing our aim is to make it an *olam*. We want it to be inviolate to prying eyes, and we endeavour to make it a fixture of secrecy. But there is one Eye from whose inquisition we can fix nothing. Unto Him all hearts are open, and from Him no secrets are hid. And this is probably the exact meaning of the psalmist when he says, Thou hast set . . . our *olams* in the light of Thy countenance.

And there was that passage from Ecclesiastes as to which the translators and revisers offered us a choice between World and Eternity—an offer that astonished us, both by its unexampled prodigality and its poverty. We can see now that what is set in the heart, or rather in the intelligence, of men is a Fixity of limitation, so that they cannot trace all that God doeth from the beginning to the end, and, consequently, cannot appreciate the beauty of His work.

A seer or a poet may say to us :—

> "God's in His heaven—
> All's right with His world,"

and we may hope it is so, and believe it is so; but we cannot always see either the process of right or the result.

Other texts not yet cited will tend to confirm the general significance we have ascribed to *olam*.

> *Psalm* cvi. 30, 31. Then stood up Phinehas and executed judgment:
> And so the plague was stayed.
> And that was counted unto him for righteousness
> Unto all generations *ad-olam* (for evermore).

Here, as has occurred before, the accepted translation commits the absurdity of making the speaker look back over endless ages, and give, so to speak, the verdict of eternity. The psalmist really employs *ad* and *olam* to point out the fixed character of the fact that the deed of Phinehas was counted to him for righteousness.

> *Lev.* xxv. 32. Nevertheless the cities of the Levites, the houses of the cities of their possession, may the Levites redeem *olam* (at any time).

In this case the use of *olam* appears to be to give fixity to a regulation: The Levites' right to redeem shall be a fixture. A tyranny of preconception as to the supposed duration-sense has put in, At any time, just as it produced Evermore in speaking of Phinehas, and Long time in telling of the silence of Jehovah and the state of the dead; but, as we see, *olam* is able to do the work set for it without our having to impose upon it such variant meanings. The regulation about the Levites' houses, the righteousness of Phinehas, the silence of Jehovah, and the condition of the dead are all alike Fixtures.

Sometimes *olam* appears in the form of *molam*, sometimes in that of *lolam;* and it is desirable the reader should note the difference between them, and how, at the same time, the change in the turn of thought, given by the prefixed letter, lends support to our Theory.

The *m* in *molam* is, as we found in speaking of *moad*, the sign of origin. It takes us back to what a thing springs from; it answers the question, Where from? If this be so, and abundant proof is at hand, then in the following words the mistranslation is obvious:—

Psalm cxix. 52. I have remembered Thy judgments *molam* (of old), O Lord,
And have comforted myself.

Of the two words chosen by the translators to interpret *molam*, the first represents the prefix *m*, and the second *olam* itself. If we ask what the judgments remembered by the psalmist spring from, the Translators' Version tells us they spring from "old." But what does that mean? It looks like a patch of fog upon the landscape. If we

OLAM AS FIXITY.

suppose them to have used the word Old in the sense of Antiquity, the intention of the psalmist is still obscured. For what comfort could he find in the fact that the judgments were merely ancient? What does help him is the remembrance of the glorious certainty of the laws of God. A judgment, or decision, of Jehovah, as, for example, that it shall be well with the righteous, is, as we say in English, of a certainty; it is from Fixity, an offspring of *olam*, and it is sure and unalterable.

In another psalm we find:—

Psalm lxxvii. 5. I have considered the days of old,
The years *molam* (of ancient times).

This looks like a repetition of a thought in different words. And what is called Hebrew parallelism is often said to be just that. It may be so sometimes, but not in the case of the greater poets; and Asaph, the author of this psalm, is one of them. By these the second sentence is generally designed to be more definite. An instance of this occurs in the well-known words, He knoweth our frame; He remembereth that we are dust. So in the quotation under consideration, The "days of old" take us back to antiquity; the "years of ancient times" put before us the characteristic of the bygone age to which reference is made. They were years *molam*; parts, or manifestations, of what is fixed and certain. But the use of this phrase, employed by other great poets besides Asaph, involves so beautiful an idea, and so important a phase of Hebrew faith, that we must leave it until we have attained to an exact knowledge of the particular shades of meaning *olam* is chosen to set forth.

G

Meanwhile I will give two other examples of the use of the form we are now examining:—

Jer. ii. 20. For *molam* (of old time) thou hast broken thy yoke.

Gen. vi. 4. The same were the mighty men which were *molam* (of old), the men of renown.

In the passage from Jeremiah the context shows that the prophet is not referring to old time at all. He is speaking to men of his own day, and of their transgressions. The fixity spoken of by *olam* refers, so far as one can see, to the truth of the statement made; and the text might read, Of a surety thou hast broken thy yoke.

This, too, would seem to be the real drift of what the historian in Genesis records of the offspring of the sons of God and the daughters of men. He is trying to emphasize the fact that they were in strength and prowess more than common; of a certainty they were mighty men, men of renown.

But, turning from *molam*, let us ask what the other form mentioned has to tell us. In *lolam* the prefixed letter is the sign of direction, tendence, or purpose. Just as *m* answers the question, Where from? so *l* answers the question, Where to? or, What for? To give an illustration a child might comprehend, if we put an *l* before Jehovah, the purport would be To Jehovah, or For Jehovah; as when we find *l* to be the original of one lot for Jehovah, and the other lot for Azazel. In other words, the purpose of *l* is to carry on our thought until it is fixed, in the illustration, upon Jehovah or upon Azazel, and, in the form *lolam*, upon *olam* itself. In this view how should we read rightly the following words?

OLAM AS FIXITY.

2 *Chron.* xxxiii. 7. And he set the graven image of the idol, which he had made, in the house of God, of which God said to David and to Solomon his son, In this house, and in Jerusalem, which I have chosen out of all the tribes of Israel, will I put My name *lolam* (for ever).

The translators make the prefix carry on our thought till it rests in perpetuity. In so doing they entail the very grave consequence that Jehovah has failed in His purpose, for the name and the house of its abode have long since and utterly vanished from Jerusalem. Indeed, at the very time to which the text refers, the name had been banished by the introduction of an idol, if by nothing else; and the writer, with the strong faith of a Jew in the immutability of Jehovah, could not have said His purpose was to put His name there For ever. But if we think of *l* as directing our attention, not to an eternal purpose, but to a fixed design, and that the sense is, I will certainly put My name there, we have a statement that accords with fact.

Here is another instance :—

Psalm xxxi 1. In Thee, O Lord, do I put my trust; let me not be ashamed *lolam* (never).

For what does the petitioner ask in this prayer? The literal meaning of the word translated Ashamed is said to be Turn Pale. Does he supplicate, then, that he may never at any time turn pale? Considering what man is, and what his world is, that would suggest itself as an impossibility. And the very next verse of the psalm shows that the author of it is pale, not to say ghastly, already! He cries out for deliverance and rescue and salvation. So we really seem to have no choice but to look upon his first petition as a prayer that his fear and his pallor may not become a fixture.

The mention of Never reminds me of an interesting distinction, a comprehension of which, although unnoticed by the English Versions, is useful in more ways than one. Readers can see no difference in the duration put into these two verses:—

Judges ii. 1. I will never break My covenant with you.

2 *Samuel* xii. 10. Now, therefore, the sword shall never depart from thy house.

In the first text the original is *lolam;* and after what has been said there will not, I think, be much difficulty in looking upon the words as a statement that God's covenant will certainly not be broken. People might look upon that as a fixture.

But in the second text, if we were to read, The sword shall certainly not depart from thy house, we should not give the true sense. We should, further, be guilty of that kind of over-coloured way of speaking which has been far too common in connection with this side of religious things. The original form in the second passage is not *lolam*, but *ad-olam*. That there is a distinction between these is obvious at a glance, and it is not at all difficult to see what it is. The first form takes us into Certainty, the second does not do so; it points to or brings Certainty into prominence as the limit or measure of what has been declared about the sword not departing from David's house. So that, while our English word Into explains *l*, we need here for the expression of *ad*'s work some such phrase as So far as, or Up to the point of. If *lolam* were the form used we should have to read, To a certainty the sword shall not depart from thy house; but seeing it is *ad-olam*, we must render, The sword shall not depart from thy house up to the point of Certainty—the sense being, Thy house will not be able to reckon upon immunity from the sword as a fixture. The Septuagint is careful to mark this distinction, and in doing so uses the Greek equivalents of the English words I have given.

There is one other instance of this mistranslation of *ad-olam* as employed in relation to punishment for sin. It is in the case of Eli :—

1 *Samuel* iii. 14. The iniquity of Eli's house shall not be purged with sacrifice nor offering for ever.

If we accepted the words as they stand we should be compelled to think of the iniquity as still unpurged after all these ages, and that it will remain unpurged to all eternity. It would require a much stronger argument than the unanimity of translators to enforce belief that a Hebrew seer, who knew what *olam* mercy means, and who did not care to speak of what he could not know, would ever put such a statement into the mouth of Jehovah. But enough has been said to show that the true purport is, The iniquity shall not, with certainty, be purged by sacrifice or offering. Nothing is said as to whether it might not be purged by other means; and in any case Never is an exaggerating interloper.

So is the member of the same fraternity in the last example to be adduced in the present chapter :—

2 *Kings* v. 27. The leprosy therefore of Naaman shall cleave unto thee, and unto thy seed *lolam* (for ever).

To say, It is fixed that Naaman's leprosy shall cleave to thee and to thy seed, may not be so "rhythmical" as, Unto thee and to thy seed for ever; but it represents what Elisha said, and that is much more to the purpose. And we need not think of Gehazi and a multitude of his progeny as lepers in some unknown world, and of others of his descendants among the inmates of lazar houses in our day, and so on through "endless ages," as we must do if the common rendering of *olam* be correct; the thought of duration is not present, and no more is averred than that the leprosy should cleave to Gehazi and his seed.

CHAPTER VIII.

OLAM
AS INVIOLABILITY AND INEVITABLENESS.

> And as it is owned the whole scheme of Scripture is not understood, so if it ever comes to be understood, before the restitution of all things and without miraculous interpositions, it must be in the same way as natural knowledge is come at ; by the continuance and progress of learning and of liberty and by particular persons attending to, comparing, and pursuing intimations scattered up and down it.
>
> BISHOP BUTLER.

HITHERTO in our pursuit of *olam* the endeavour has been simply to mark and confirm the general sense of the word. The reader will, however, have noticed that in some instances *olam* has been indicative of Stability, and in others of Certainty, and it is to these specific meanings that our attention must now be directed. The best terms, as it seems to me, by which to describe them are the words Inviolate and Inevitable. A thing is stable really because it is inviolate to all that can be thought of as tending to make it other than it is, the inviolacy being relative or absolute according to the nature of what is spoken of. And an event is properly said to be certain when it is inevitable, when it is, so to speak, invincible to all that can be imagined as possibly preventing its occurrence.

We shall find that in some cases *olam* has both these

meanings. In others it is not always easy to say which sense is to be preferred, while, at the same time, it may be of the greatest importance to be able to decide. But there can be little doubt that *olam* will always, in every instance of its use, be interpreted in accordance with what has been said about its general meaning of Fixity, or the particular phases of Fixity spoken of as Inviolability and Inevitableness, and never by anything else.

As instances of the necessity of giving to *olam* the general meaning of Fixity and, on looking closer, both of the special meanings, I may quote the following texts:—

Isaiah xlv. 17. But Israel shall be saved in the Lord with *olam* (everlasting) salvation.

Hosea ii. 19. And I will betroth thee unto Me *lolam* (for ever); yea, I will betroth thee unto Me in righteousness, and in judgment, and in loving-kindness, and in mercies.

In the passage from Isaiah *olam* declares the Salvation of Israel, in Jehovah, to be a fixed thing. If we ask in what sense it is a fixity the answer is plain: It is inevitable, sure to be; and further, the Salvation, when accomplished, will be inviolate to all antagonistic and destructive influences, or it would neither be Salvation nor *olam*. So it is with the Betrothal of which the other prophet speaks. It also is *olam* in the two-fold sense—nothing can prevent it, and nothing will be able to break it.

We shall all begin to be interested by these distinctive meanings when we go on to inquire how they apply in such a statement as this from the Book of Ecclesiastes:—

Ecclesiastes xii. 5. Man goeth to his *beth-olam* (long home).

This reminds us of the *beth-moad*, the appointed and

prominent house to which we are all journeying. Here we have the same house spoken of as the *olam* or fixed house. In what sense is it a fixture? It is curious that both *ad* and *olam*, so often in our English Bible turned into For ever, should be used to qualify that of which no Christian interpreter would ever consent to say it is everlasting. The House of the Dead is *olam*, fixed in the sense of inevitable. That is clear enough and demonstrable. Does anyone feel inclined to go on and say the *beth-olam* is also fixed in the sense of being inviolate? Some men do say so, and with confidence. But that is not to talk in the fashion of the Hebrew seers. It would be to declare that the grave will never be disturbed, that there is no exit on the other side, that from this bourn *no* traveller returns; in short, it would be to assert all sorts of unprovable things. What the author of the saying does state is the fact that man goeth to his inevitable home, and of the truth of that declaration there can be no denial.

By way of contrast I will cite a case in which the other word is as plainly to be preferred :—

Isaiah xxxii. 17-19. And the work of righteousness shall be peace, and the effect of righteousness quietness and assurance *ad-olam* (for ever). And My people shall dwell in a peaceable habitation, and in sure dwellings, and in quiet resting-places, when it shall hail, coming down on the forest; and the city shall be low in a low place.

That *ad-olam* is intended to convey the idea of *up to the point of Inviolacy*, and not merely that of Certainty, is seen from what follows it. The quietness and assurance will not be invaded. There will be hail on the forest, and the city will be abased, but the dwellings of My People will be invulnerable; they will be peaceable, and sure and quiet.

Something was said of a thing being absolutely or only relatively inviolate according to the circumstances of the case. As an instance of the latter, let us recur to that queer-looking exclamation of the Eastern courtier, O king, live for ever! It is really not so foolish as it looks. One may see now that it cannot mean either O king, may you never die, or, O king, may you live inevitably; *olam* speaks of such inviolability as in the nature of the case is possible. It looks at the life of the king reaching on to a natural and peaceful conclusion, and expresses a wish that it may be shielded from evil—inviolate to the assassin and to the invasions of pain and want.

The next examples, though treating of much the same topic, afford us a contrast to this Eastern salutation:—

Job vii. 16. I would not live *lolam* (alway).

Gen. iii. 22. And now lest he put forth his hand and take of the tree of life and eat, and live *lolam* (for ever).

We are so accustomed to take the obscurities and other curiosities of language in the English Bible without reflection, that if the translators had rendered *olam* in the first of these extracts as they have done in the second, and made Job say, I would not live for ever, we should perhaps have accepted the reading without surprise. But the translators were aware that Job gave some indication of hope in a life to come, and they could not make him contradict himself. The dominating idea that *olam* implies Duration set them hunting among English words, until at length they lit upon Alway. Under the circumstances the choice is a very good one, and suggests the sense, if it does not exactly express it. Job means that he would not have his life, in its present condition, inviolate to Death. His flesh is clothed with worms, his days are spent without hope; so he would choose strangling rather than life. To have such an existence fixed, invulnerable to death, is a thought intolerable.

The saying quoted from the story of Eden is one of so much difficulty that any earnest effort at solution will involve an aching of the faculties. I have an opinion about its meaning, but am not above changing it, if reason can be shown. The problem itself may easily be seen. The *l* in *lolam* takes us on to—what? It cannot be to Certainty, or Inevitableness, as though we should read, Lest he eat, and live to a certainty, for it has been fixed that Adam shall die. Nor can it carry us on to Inviolability in the sense that the life shall be invulnerable to sorrow and pain, and toil and death. These "evils" have already been announced, and it is not to be supposed that the Tree of Life, whatever that may mean, could confer immunity from them.

The key to the meaning seems to be in the fact that there was something to fear. This was not the possibility that man could make himself immortal, or that he could escape any part of the consequences of his act; that, as we can all see, was out of the question. But if that is the case it would seem the only cause for apprehension was lest the condition into which man had fallen should itself be a fixity in the sense of being impervious to all ameliorative influences, lest, that is to say, the woman's subjection and her sorrow, the man's toil and the death awaiting both, should be unmitigated.

It would need a lengthy disquisition on the meaning

of the Tree of Life, and, indeed, on that of the whole story, to show how one is warranted in coming to this conclusion. But, let us ask, what has history and experience to say on the point? The New Woman and her followers would perhaps object, but most others would agree with the opinion of St. Paul, that it is not altogether an unhappy thing for a woman to be in subjection to a husband; and when she is asked if she will accept such a position her reply is, I will. And again we are told—and the New Woman herself does not appear to deny this—that notwithstanding the pangs and the dangers of childbirth, all women who love their lords are quite willing to undergo them for the sake of the joys of motherhood, and are even said to be disappointed if they have not the opportunity. As to toil, there is a perennial nobleness and even sacredness in work. One of the great lessons of life is the value of labour and the evil of the want of it. And the last part of Adam's doom, death, is not all an evil any more than the rest. We are taught how dreadful a thing it is to die, and people are afraid of it—till it comes. Then, as anyone who has seen many death-beds will testify, it is usually as natural and as welcome as sleep.

All this appears to me to be put in another way by what is said of the Cherubim and the pointed flame placed at the gate of Eden to keep the way of the tree of life. Adam and his wife are outside of Eden; and the way back is through the fiery trial, and the holy dignity of what has been imposed upon them. They have eaten of the tree of the knowledge *of the good of evil*. Let them carry that out to its consequences. The path to Paradise for the woman is in subjection to her husband and in motherhood; in the opportunities afforded by those conditions to what is most divine in her there are possibilities of a worthier Eden than that which has been forfeited. The way for man is in the sweat of brow and brain. Think of what that has done since Adam began to delve! And the man who is conscious that by painful labour he, like his God, has done something to make life on earth more tolerable, more attractive, more noble, finds the gate of Paradise, whose Keeper says, Well done! And if we remember the different senses in which the words Living and Dying are used in Scripture, we shall see how the Christian doctrine and painful process of dying in order to live is also illustrated by this ancient conception of Eden's gate. The whole picture is, in fact, a presentation of the straight and narrow way of duty which is the path to glory. And, so seen, it is one of the many interesting testimonies to the real unity of Scripture.

"No way to Eden, now, save through the fire,"

is only another way of saying, Through much tribulation we enter the Kingdom of God.

But it may be thought that we are not only straying from the direct course of word-exposition, but are also becoming fanciful. The point is the true meaning of *olam;* and in this text about Eden it certainly does not signify For ever, any more than it does elsewhere. Whether we take the narrative as historical or as poetical, *olam* stands for Fixity in the sense of Inviolability.

So it does in another text from Genesis, almost as difficult as the foregoing :—

Genesis vi. 3. My Spirit shall not strive with man *lolam* (always), for that he also is flesh; yet his days shall be a hundred and twenty years.

If we were to read, My Spirit shall not strive with man to a certainty, or inevitably, we should contradict what we believe to be fact. On the other hand, we cannot consent to see in the words an acknowledgment on the part of Deity of the inefficacy of His Spirit. And there is no need. The text really suggests that man, being flesh as well as spirit, often needs something besides spirit in God's dealings with him. *Olam* points to Fixity in the sense of Invincibility. What we mean by Spirit is not invincible as against what we understand by Flesh. Flesh must feel the force of flood and fire; it must be delivered over to Satan for destruction, that the spirit may be saved. So that here again we have thus early in the Bible an indication of modes of thought common to its writers in later ages.

The way of the Spirit, the way to Eden, comes before us in the following beautiful prayer from one of the psalms :—

Psalm cxxxix. 23, 24. Search me, O God, and know my heart;
Try me, and know my thoughts;
And see if there be any wicked way in me,
And lead me in the way *olam* (everlasting).

The Hebrew word in this quotation rendered Wicked is the same that in the story of Eden meets us in the form of sorrow: I will greatly multiply the sorrow of thy conception. One of the commentators says it includes all the troubles associated with child-birth — labour, pain, difficulty, and danger. Does the psalmist pray that he may be free from these? We should have to think he did so if we took the force of *olam* to be absolute inviolability. But no Biblical psalmist would ask to be led in a way inviolate to all pain and labour, and difficulty and danger. Such a path would have attractions for many people, but not for a seer; he knew the best path must be a *via crucis*, that a Son of God must be perfected through sufferings.

The fact is, the word translated Sorrow is also one of the picturesque terms chosen by Hebrew writers to express what they thought of idolatry. It was a prolific source of labour and pain, as Israelites too often proved. Once we know this, we can see that the psalmist is asking that any tendency of the kind in himself may be detected, and that he may be led in a path inviolate to the pangs caused by forsaking Jehovah. To call it, as the translators do, the way everlasting is no doubt to give it one of its proper titles, but it is also, if I may so speak, to miss the light that illuminates the path.

Isaiah, with whose book we shall, in the remainder of our survey, be largely occupied, gives us an amusing instance of the use of *olam*, one, too, that shows the justness of our theory, search in what quarter we may:—

Isaiah xlvii. 7. Thou saidst, I shall be a lady *lolam* (for ever).

The text means no less than, I shall certainly be a lady, and a lady inviolate. What is a lady *olam?* Probably, if pressed for an answer to the question we should give varying definitions. The "lady" who speaks in the quotation, and who, in other language, is called The virgin daughter of Babylon, has a very clear idea of her own. To be a lady is not to have to work like a slave at grinding corn and carrying water. It is also to be a wife and mother, and never to sit as a widow, or know the loss of children. In short, to be an *olam* lady was to live a life inviolate to the evils which women in those days most dreaded.

But the virgin daughter of Babylon had not trodden the narrow way. She had not been merciful; even upon the aged she had put a heavy yoke. And Isaiah says her certainty is a delusion, her inviolacy will be invaded. She will have to take the millstones, and grind meal; she will be compelled to remove the veil, strip off the train, uncover the leg, and wade through the rivers. And, as to her fancied immunity from other ills, these two things shall come upon her in one day—the loss of children and widowhood!

All this apparently discursive talk, and flitting from place to place in search of the manifold uses of *olam*, has been preparatory to an object that has never been lost sight of. This is, partly, to arrive at a precise apprehension of the exact meaning of the word in such texts as the following :—

Isaiah xxxiv. 10. It shall not be quenched night nor day; the smoke thereof shall go up *lolam* (for ever).

Jer. xvii. 4. Ye have kindled a fire in mine anger which shall burn *ad-olam* (for ever).

Jer. xx. 11. An *olam* (everlasting) confusion that shall never be forgotten.

Daniel xii. 2. And many of them that sleep in the dust of the earth shall awake, some to *olam* (everlasting) life, and some to shame and *olam* (everlasting) contempt.

Jer. li. 39. I will make drunk her princes, and her wise men, her governors and her deputies, and her mighty men ; and they shall sleep an *olam* (everlasting) sleep, and not wake, saith the King, whose name is the Lord of Hosts.

The important work before us in reviewing these quotations is to discover, if possible, whether *olam* is used in the sense of Inevitableness or in that of Inviolability. If the former is the purport, then there can be no question that we are misled by the translators' employment of For ever and Everlasting; for it does not at all follow that because a thing is spoken of as inevitable it is also everlasting. But if *olam* in these texts has the significance of Inviolability, the translators may be justified in using terms expressive of endless duration for the reason that everlastingness may be the result of a thing being inviolate, just as we have seen a thing may be hidden as a consequence of its being fixed from sight. The result of our inquiry will not greatly affect our theory; for if it should turn out that Everlasting is correct, it can only be so in a secondary and consequent sense; the primary meaning of *olam* would still be seen to be Fixity. But the investigation is necessary on other grounds, and chiefly that it may prepare us for the study of similar texts in the New Testament.

Some of the passages in the list need not detain us. No one will think that Jeremiah intended to speak of a literal never-ending slumber. In Daniel's saying there are reasons why we should think of the *olam* life as inviolate, and the *olam* contempt as inevitable. But those reasons will be more in place in the New Testament discussions. Of the two other quotations from Jeremiah, the first says, The fire *ad-olam* shall burn; and there is no reason why we should think the prophet means more than that what he says will inevitably come to pass. In the second text the translators give us two indications of endless duration where there is no necessity for us to see any. The original is simply, An *olam* confusion, not forgotten. Isaiah's words need a more careful and extended scrutiny.

If Isaiah had said no more than, The smoke thereof shall go up *lolam*, there would be no reason for us to think he meant more than, The smoke thereof shall go up to a certainty. But he also says, It shall not be quenched night nor day; and from this it is certain he was thinking, not only of an inevitable fire, but also of a fire inviolate to all antagonistic influence, a fire that should not be quenched.

Hence we have seriously to consider whether the fire may not rightly be thought of as everlasting as the consequence of its being inviolate. The interest of the question is felt when we allow our thoughts to go on for a moment to the New Testament books, written by the same race of men as the authors of the Old Testament, and think of the everlasting or eternal fire that is spoken of in them.

I think the inquiry will be found to resolve itself into the query whether Isaiah speaks of absolute or only of relative inviolacy. That he does speak of the fire as being superior to all endeavour to quench it that he can think of cannot be doubted; whether he conceives of it as being altogether and absolutely invulnerable and unquenchable is another question. I venture to think he did not, and that, as a seer, he could not.

Absolute or partial inviolacy must depend upon the nature of a thing; and it will help us here to turn to examples of the latter, and see why it would be a misuse of language to speak of them as Everlasting. The reader will remember the *olam* landmark. In the thought and intention of those who set it up it was to be inviolate, but no seer would have called it Eternal. Landmarks are inviolate, subject to the changes in time, authority, and custom. Israel was at one time an *olam* people; in after years they were not so. Their inviolacy was conditioned by their faithfulness. Jehovah brought an *olam* nation in war against them; a nation inviolate or invincible for the purpose in view, but not therefore an everlasting nation. A slave, again, could not be a bondman "for ever," but only until old age or death brought the servitude to an end. To say that a landmark shall be everlastingly a landmark, or a slave eternally a slave, is to say what no seer could see, and what, as a matter of fact, no seer ever has said.

We have heard Isaiah speak of doomed places, which were to be *olam* dens; not dens for ever, as the translators put it, but *olam* dens until the pouring out of the Spirit. Another text from the same prophet very much to the point is:—

Isaiah lviii. 12. And they that shall be of thee shall build the *olam* (ancient) waste places.

The waste places were deserts, or perhaps ruins, whose desolation to ordinary eyes was inviolate or inveterate. But it was not so really, not absolutely. There was a time when most people would have said of the salt deseit of Utah, It is an *olam* waste. But even then there were not wanting keen-sighted men who could predict of it, so far at least as the physical aspect went, The wilderness and the solitary place shall be glad; the desert shall rejoice and blossom as the rose.

And no man loving truth, and evincing that love in his use of language, could ever speak of a desert of any kind as eternal; for the desolation depends upon certain causes, and whether they are inveterate or not we cannot say. But to speak of it as everlasting is to imply a knowledge on our part that the climatic or other causes of sterility will be endlessly permanent. How can we, how can a seer even, attain to the knowledge of that?

This reasoning seems to hold good in the case of Isaiah's smoke and fire, and the wrath of God, of which they are thought to speak. He says the smoke will inevitably go up, that the fire will burn inviolate, invincible, to all attempts to quench it, yet he does not say the fire will be everlasting. I think the reader will be able to satisfy himself that the prophet could not aver any such thing. His business is to speak of what is demonstrable. He knows that in Jehovah, in the perfect Love, there must be ebullitions and activities of what we call anger; and he knows that Jehovah, being God, nothing on the part of men, nothing of which we can conceive, can stay or check His wrath. So that in the general sense of the word, and in both its specific meanings, the seer can declare the wrath of God to be *olam;* but beyond that he cannot go. Wrath, like fire, is contingent; like the desolation of the desert, it depends on certain causes, and no man can say the causes will be eternal.

So far as I can find, no Biblical writer or speaker, either in the Old or the New Testament, has ever attributed endless duration to fire or to the Divine anger. Thinking, as I am obliged to think, of revelation as bringing things to our knowledge, and that we cannot *know* what is incapable of proof, I do not see how they could. Led by the seers, we can all see, if we will, that the wrath of God against wrong must inevitably burn, and that when He ariseth to shake terribly the earth none can hinder; but that is a very different thing from saying that He who lit the fire will never see cause to suppress it, or that the fire itself will never go out for lack of fuel.

Absolute inviolability may not, then, be used of wrath. For wrath is a thing caused, and therefore contingent. But when the Hebrew prophets speak of Love, they know, as we shall have abundant opportunity of showing, they are dealing with essence, and not with attribute. Love Divine, all loves excelling, is uncaused and unconditioned. Hence *olam* can be applied to it in the utmost sense of absolute inviolacy.

Isaiah liv. 8. In overflowing wrath I hid My face from thee for a moment; but with *olam* kindness will I have mercy on thee, saith the Lord thy Redeemer.

Yes, the wrath is overflowing, it is like the Flood. To us and our sight, so easily filled, it may well seem absolute, infinite, endless; but to the prophet it is not so. He knows what is, and must be, behind the frowning providence: I hid My face from thee for a moment, but with *olam* kindness will I have mercy on thee. And lest we should be in danger of confounding such an *olam* as this with *olams* of limited inviolability, like Sinai, or Carmel, or Lebanon, he goes on to say: The mountains shall depart, and the hills be removed; but My kindness shall not depart from thee, neither shall My covenant of peace be removed, saith Jehovah, who hath mercy upon thee.

CHAPTER IX.

THE OLAM GOD.

Jehovah, the *olam* God, Creator of the Ends of the Earth, fainteth not, neither is weary.

IN the early pages of the preceding chapter a saying was quoted and left over for consideration until we should be in a position to read it with appreciation. The words were :—

Psalm lxxvii. 5. I have considered the days of old,
     The years *molam* (of ancient times).

To this we may now add two other texts—one from Moses and one from Isaiah :—

Deut. xxxii. 7. Remember the days *olam* (of old).

Isaiah li. 9. Awake, awake, put on strength, O arm of the Lord, awake as in the days of old, the generations *olam* (of ancient times).

Looking at these passages as they stand in English, we have three of the greatest of Hebrew poets talking in a tautological and unmeaning fashion. Two of them, at least, appear to say the same thing over again in different words. Asaph says, I have considered the days of old; and when we naturally expect him to tell us what he saw in the Days of Old that was remarkable, he simply has nothing to say, except that they were Years of Ancient Times. Isaiah cries to the Arm of the Lord to awake as in the days of old; and when we want to know what the awaking of the Arm was like in those days, he says no more than, The generations of ancient times. The quotations take us back to bygone times, and then leave us wondering why we were brought there! In the course of this chapter we shall have to quote from modern English poets, who could not be allowed, much less made, to occupy us with that kind of thing; and a terrible injustice has been done to the ancient bards in disguising their thoughts by senseless language.

As was previously intimated, the second line in what is called Hebrew Parallelism is, in the greater poets, often intended as an amplification, or explanation, of the drift of the first line. So here the Days of Old are defined as Years *molam* and Generations *olam;* that is, in view of our interpretation of *olam*, they were years and generations of Fixity or Certainty. But we must remember we are dealing with poetry, and that Generations, Years, and Days are not used in rigid and prosaic fashion. A "generation" of Fixity is that which is brought into being, or activity, by Fixity. "Days" and "years" of Fixity are times, or occasions, in which Fixity was manifested. Thus when Asaph says he has pondered the days of old, he goes on to tell us that he refers to the time when Fixity was manifested. And Isaiah cries to the Arm of Jehovah to awake, as it did in those long past ages when it brought certainties into activity.

Before we go on to make ourselves acquainted with the peculiar phase of religious thought to which these texts will bring us there is an all-important saying of Isaiah's which must first be noticed :—

Isaiah xlvi. 9. Remember the former things *molam* (of old); for I am God and none else.

The text appears to have a connection with the others; so it has, but not just as may probably be anticipated. If we take it word for word, and try to re-state it in clearer language, its appearance will be startling, especially to an Agnostic, who prefers to speak of God as unknowable. The word Remember will do very well, if we bear in mind that to remember a thing is to bring it into present view. The Former Things must be altered to The Chief, or Foremost, Things. *Molam*, as by this time we can have no doubt, is Of Certainty, or From Fixity. The first part of the text thus reads, Keep in view the foremost things of Certainty. The plural number is a Hebrew peculiarity often found in connection with a thing or a person of which we should speak as singular. But we want to know what this First of Certainties is. If we look at the text again, and change the For into That, as it ought to be changed, we shall have the answer. Jehovah is the Speaker, and the Chief of Fixities is that He is God, or Supreme, and none else.

I hinted that the language of Isaiah would, when clearly understood, startle an Agnostic; but his statement is enough to agitate many an orthodox believer. For it says, in effect, that Jehovah does not wish His existence and His nature to be taken upon trust, or to be believed in simply. Jehovah is the First of Certainties; and we cannot know that anything is certain unless its certainty can be verified.

But, leaving this for the present, the reader will now be able to see what the three poets, Moses, Asaph, and Isaiah, really saw in the old days to which they refer. They looked back to those days as being the time when He whom Isaiah calls the Foremost Certainty manifested Himself in activities that were afterwards looked upon and spoken of as From Fixity.

As everyone will surmise, those days could be none other than the time of Israel's redemption and education. The Burning Bush, the overthrow of Egypt, the path through deep waters, the Manna, the desert stream, the Law, and the Inheritance—these, to Moses and the others, were manifestations, not of occasional or transient acts of lovingkindness, but of what is fixed and always. And this is that phase of Jewish faith to which reference was made a while since.

All this will be evident if we look at the quotations under review in the light of their context.

Moses, having called upon the people to remember the Days *olam*, proceeds to enumerate the characteristics of those "days":—

> The Lord's portion is His people;
> Jacob is the lot of His inheritance.
> He found him in the desert land,
> And in the waste howling wilderness;
> He compassed him about, He cared for him,
> He kept him as the apple of His eye:
> As an eagle that stirreth up her nest,
> That fluttereth over her young,
> He spread abroad His wings, He took them,
> He bare them on His pinions:
> The Lord alone did lead him,
> And there was no strange god with him.

And this to Moses was a manifestation of what is fixed. What Jehovah did once He will do always. The Song goes on to tell of unfaithfulness and rebellion and idolatry on the part of Israel, and the resulting troubles. But even then the truth that Jehovah alone delivers is taught by the experience that there is no redemption out of Him. And when things are at their worst the poet's insight can sing :—

> I would make the remembrance of them to cease from among men,
> Were it not that I feared the provocation of the enemy.

The words sound strange to us, and it is a way of putting things that we perhaps should not choose, but the meaning is, I cannot give thee up. And by-and-by when all false gods have been proved false, the Song ends with a summons to the nations to rejoice because of vengeance on the adversaries and mercy for Israel.

Asaph, as his psalm shows, is full of his own troubles. He is in sorrow and doubt; his spirit is overwhelmed. Then he looks back to the years *molam*, and sings the deeds of Jehovah :—

> Thy way was in the sea,
> And Thy paths in the great waters,
> And Thy footsteps were not known.
> Thou leddest Thy people like a flock
> By the hand of Moses and Aaron.

The argument is: Jehovah is what He was there, for He is unchangeable. How, then, could I think He hath forgotten to be gracious? That I should fear His failure was my infirmity. I cannot see Him at His work, but that makes no difference. Who could see Him in the

Exodus? Men saw nothing but storm and lightning and leaping waves. His footsteps were not known. Yet all the time He was leading Israel like a flock, and—He must be leading me.

Isaiah is most of all taken, as was Asaph, with the *olam* shown in the vanquishing of Egypt and the passage through the Sea. After his appeal to the Arm of the Lord to awake, as in the generations *olam*, he very plainly gives us to understand what he has in his mind in making use of the expression :—

> Art Thou not it [the Arm] that cut Rahab in pieces, that pierced the dragon?
> Art Thou not it which dried up the sea, the waters of the great deep;
> That made the depths of the sea a way for the ransomed to pass over?

This, in the prophet's mind, was an *olam;* it was a manifestation of what is fixed and inviolate. Consequently it will occur again, and always. The generations *olam* were momentary drawing-asides of the veil which hides from human sight what is inviolately fixed and inevitably sure. So Isaiah can follow on his words with a Therefore :—

> Therefore the redeemed of Jehovah shall return, and come with singing unto Zion;
> And *olam* joy shall be upon their heads:
> They shall obtain gladness and joy,
> And sorrow and sighing shall flee away.

Thus we see these poets to be worthy of the name. They do not take us back to dim ages and leave us to ask in vain why we have been brought there. They picture to us scenes of wonder, and tell us we look upon revelations of what is *olam;* and they bid us believe, as one of our own bards has done, that:—

> One adequate support
> For the calamities of mortal life
> Exists—one only; an assured belief
> That the procession of our fate, howe'er
> Sad or disturbed, is ordered by a Being
> Of infinite benevolence and power;
> Whose everlasting purposes embrace
> All accidents, converting them to good.

One or two thoughts will arise here, and they require notice, although they may detain us for the moment from our more immediate purpose. To speak of Jehovah as a Certainty is to say that whatever is understood by that word is capable of demonstration. This is to assume a position and to use language utterly at variance with that of some more modern ecclesiastic authorities. They tell us we must, as a first requisite, lay aside such faculties as we have and accept whatever wonder may be declared to us without question and without doubt. The method of the Hebrew seer—and who can hesitate to believe which method will ultimately prevail?—is to challenge us to make use of our powers in testing and proving. He says, I offer something to you, not to your speculation, not to your thought or belief only, but to your *knowledge;* and to knowledge that is properly so called, the knowledge which comes of experiment and demonstration. It is this: Jehovah is an *olam* God; He is inviolably supreme.

Of course, the question comes, What did the seer mean by Jehovah? Fully to answer the question would require a volume to itself. It must suffice to say here that St. John, who is pictured to us as receiving part of his education at the voice of Moses and in the light of the Shechinah glory, could not have a different idea of God from that of the older prophets. And he tells us that to make a deity of love and to abide in love is for a man to abide in the Supreme, and to have the Supreme abiding in him. So Moses says Jehovah is what alone can be loved with all the heart and mind, and soul and strength, of which a human being is capable; and Jehovah is what sets him loving his neighbour as he loves himself. Whether the Hebrew conceived of Jehovah as a person, in the sense of the Athanasian Creed, he does not tells us. One feels sure that if the seer were told Jehovah was a person he would immediately ask, What kind of person? and especially in heart and purpose? For the seer loved definite and informing language; and he preferred to speak of Jehovah as the Sun and Shield, and as *olam* Rock, and *olam* Light, and *olam* Love. And these are not only clear and informing definitions, they are open to demonstration.

Another point may perhaps be raised by readers who do not think that miracles happen. That story of the Exodus and the wonders of the journey—if we cannot accept them as having actually occurred as reported, what becomes of their supposed revelations of matters of certainty? From all I can learn, I think a Hebrew teacher would have been surprised that such a question could be asked, and not a little indignant also. As Jesus would have been had any one said to Him, Did that case of the prodigal ever happen? if not, how can we know God is like that father? History is not the only vehicle of truth. The Hebrew prophet would, as was his manner, turn the matter round upon the questioner. He would, I think, say, This is a thing you may know and prove: Jehovah is such that the thought of Him, faith in Him, and loving allegiance to Him, will infallibly result in redemption from all bondage, in water from the rock, and manna in the desert, in safe journeying to a land flowing with milk and honey; go thou and try. And at least one thing will be clear to us all, that until we have tried we have no right to say Jehovah is not what He is proclaimed to us as being.

But, to get back again into the direct course of our business, when Isaiah has told us that Jehovah is the First of Certainties we have not heard all he has to say by a very great deal. Here is another quotation from his book:—

Isaiah xl. 28. Hast thou not known, hast thou not heard, that the *olam* (everlasting) God, the Lord, the Creator of the ends of the earth, fainteth not, neither is weary?

The revisers, in their margin, suggest The Lord is an everlasting God as an alternative to the reading of the older version. Isaiah wrote, Jehovah is an *olam* God. And I think these words require no less a sense than that of Inviolate Supremacy. And, indeed, the whole of the immortal fortieth chapter is nothing less than a picture of Jehovah's inviolable supremacy, or, to use other words having the same meaning, His absolute indefectibility. The skill and resource with which Isaiah marshals things and events, and wants and difficulties, as possibly militating against the supremacy of Jehovah in human thought, is one

THE OLAM GOD.

of the most marvellous achievements even in Hebrew literature. But it is his argument with which we are concerned here; and that is, Jehovah is an *olam* God.

In this almost the only place where the epithet Everlasting is fitting how poor a word really it is seen to be. Almost any god, and, for the matter of that, almost any thing, might conceivably be thought of as everlasting. The word, when we scrutinize it, has little or nothing to tell us of character, nothing whatever of mind or capacity, or heart or purpose. But the word of the prophet, *olam*, tells us all! To say Jehovah is the *olam* Supreme is revelation indeed.

I will venture here to quote lines which have been of service to myself. They are brought in not because of any poetic merit, but because I believe them to give a concise account of Isaiah's argument and a true and full definition of *olam*.

" God were not *olam* if the depth or height
   Of wilderness obstructed His career;
   Or if His word no longer taught the seer;
If any sheep could wander in the night,
Or fall a victim to an alien might;
   If thought of ours could counsel at His ear,
   Or better frame, or better guide, a sphere,
   Or set the counterpart of God in sight!
   And He must keep the utmost stars in call;
Control the devious path by Israel trod;
Hear, and interpret, every dumb complaint;
And but to think of HIM must cheer the faint!
   Or He could not be *olam* over all:
So—Comfort ye My people, saith your God."

It is very pathetic to see, as we give another glance at Isaiah's great chapter, the poor godmaker choosing gold, or, if that be beyond him, then at least a tree *that will not rot*, out of which to fashion his deity. May one not say it is a divine instinct that bids him choose what is most precious and most enduring? What strikes Isaiah is that such a god, even when all of gold, has to be chained up to the wall to keep it from falling down; and when there is need that it should change its position it has to be carried.

It must make all the difference to any man if the god whom he worships can only be kept in place by chains of any kind. We want a god who will keep us in place— one who depends upon us, or others, or anything, for a throne is not *olam*. Or, to use Isaiah's other illustration, we do not want a god whom we are obliged to carry, and who is a burden to us. And indeed the days are coming when men will no longer consent to stagger about beneath such unnatural loads as these. Men, in Bible language, are sheep; and the essential need of sheep is a shepherd to feed them, not a shepherd whom they must feed. The poor things would have nothing to offer him (except grass), and nothing to offer it with. And we men, we want a god who will carry us, and make a continual burden of us, and never faint or be weary. And this is what the *olam* God of Isaiah does: Even to hoar hairs will I carry you: I have made, and I will bear; yea, I will carry, and will deliver. (xlvi. 4.)

Seeing all this, how

> "God's greatness rolls around our incompleteness,
> Around our restlessness His rest,"

we cease to wonder at the strong and confident language

THE OLAM GOD.

in which the Bible seers speak of Jehovah. They exhort men to hope in Him with inviolable confidence. They call upon all that is within them to declare His worth and to praise the unique Name. Their writings are jubilant with doxologies singing of His glory and honour as the certainty of certainties. They literally dance with joy before Him; like boys breaking into the brightness of holiday, they seem to throw up their caps as they cry, Shout unto Jehovah, all the earth! and the very trees of the field are made to clap their hands with ecstasy at the thought that Love inviolate shall judge the world.

One more text from Isaiah will help us to understand what in the mouth of an Israelite was meant by His mercy is *olam* :—

Isaiah xxvi. 4. Trust ye in Jehovah *ady-ad* (for ever): for in the Lord Jehovah is rock *olam* (everlasting strength).

What, let us ask, is rock *olam* ? After all our study we shall conclude it can be nothing less than rock inviolable; that is to say, rock which cannot be removed or shattered, or broken or crumbled or corroded. Rock it must be that is invulnerable to everything that can be thought of as ordinarily destructive of its nature. So light *olam* is light that cannot be dimmed or eclipsed or extinguished, or even outshone. Do we recognize the full bearing of this upon the Divine Mercy? There are forces antagonistic to mercy and ordinarily destructive of it, such as wilful and reiterated wrong-doing, base ingratitude, cruel rebellion, and black treachery; but the Mercy of Jehovah is *olam*, it is absolutely inviolable! This is what the Israelite meant by his chant, familiar to us in the form of His Mercy endureth For ever.

True, his ideas of mercy may have differed from our own. Our prayer, Have Mercy upon me, perhaps, means no more than Let me off from punishment. To the Hebrew Mercy belongs to Jehovah, because He rewardeth every man according to his works. But it is Love, nevertheless, or, rather, all the more. *Olam* Love, indefectible as well as inviolable; Love bearing all things, faithful in all things, hoping all things, enduring all things; Love that never faileth.

Enduring all things. In a noble book, too little known—*The Gospel of Divine Humanity*—there is a Hindoo fable which tells of a man who made up his mind to test the patience of God by striking Him. He does so, and is met by the gentle remark, I am afraid you have hurt yourself. Yes, we hurt ourselves; but, according to the Hebrew seers, we cannot injure, or alter, or lessen the mercy of God. We may be sure of it now, and sure of it at the last.

If love be the first of *olams* all difficulties must yield to it, as Isaiah saw in his fortieth chapter. And not Isaiah alone. In the psalm I am about to quote imagination, or the lack of it, may see in the doors it mentions a reference to the Temple gates. But they would hardly be thought of as *olam*, especially at the approach of Him whose dwelling-place was there. There are other "doors," we can all think of them, which are shut to Jehovah, closed against love, and some of them seem inviolably shut. But they are not so. Hills are scattered, and the *olam* mountains bow at God's approach, and bolts and bars in human minds and hearts will be withdrawn when the cry to men is understood:—

Psalm xxiv. 7, 8.   Lift up your heads, O ye gates;
And be ye lift up, ye *olam* doors:
And the KING OF GLORY shall come in.

This may be spoken of as Jehovah in invincible attack upon what is apparently impregnable. But there are not wanting pictures of His invincibility in defence. I will quote the most delightful of all:—

Deuteronomy xxxiii. 27.   The eternal God is thy refuge;
And underneath are the *olam* arms.

This beautiful figure occurs in the dying words of Moses, of whom it was said that he talked with Jehovah face to face. Can anything surpass it as gospel for men? We may think the arms of motherhood the most inviolate defence, but they are not. The babe may be snatched from her breast by stronger force, or it may sicken and die there; nay, her arms may relax, sometimes not altogether involuntarily, and the child fall to the ground. The seers noted this defect, and its lesson: Can a woman forget her sucking child, that she should not have compassion on the son of her womb? Yea, these may forget, yet will I not forget thee.

O fellow-men, belief in the *olam* God, what a creed it is! Here was a man who knew Jehovah as none before him had done, who had, so to speak, discovered Him, and named and proclaimed Him to men. He spent many years in His service and lived in His presence, and when he died his eye was not dim nor his natural strength abated. And this is his dying message to sinners like ourselves. In danger and in weariness, at the coming of storm and mysterious night, and especially when the world is receding, and heart and flesh are failing, he would have us say:—

> "Safe in Thine arms I lay me down,
> The arms, inviolate, of love."

The old dogma of inspiration, of the supernatural communication to the human mind of truth beyond its unassisted power to see, appears to be a good deal shaken in these days. If it should altogether go, these Hebrew poets will have to be accorded that highest rank as men of genius of which the doctrine in question has perhaps tended to deprive them. For is there in literature anything, at all events on the greatest of subjects, anything to compare with what I have tried to reproduce from the Hebrew Bible?

It is singular, in some aspects, that several of our own modern poets should have reached the same conclusion as the Hebrews. It would not be respectful to say they borrowed from the Bible, and I think there are sufficient reasons of another kind for believing that they gained what they give us as their vision of the truth independently of the Hebrew Scriptures. Here is a well-known, almost hackneyed, quotation from Pope:—

> "All Nature is but art, unknown to thee;
> All chance, direction, which thou canst not see;
> All discord, harmony, not understood;
> All partial evil, universal good:
> And spite of pride, in erring reason's spite,
> One truth is clear, whatever is, is right"

This may be followed by the equally well-known words of Tennyson, teaching not quite so confidently the same lesson :—

> "That nothing walks with aimless feet;
> And not one life shall be destroyed,
> Or cast as rubbish to the void,
> When God hath made the pile complete."

But a contribution from Browning is, as I think, much more welcome, for the reason that it supplies argument, and not statement only :—

> "Do I find love so full in my nature, God's ultimate gift,
> That I doubt His own love can compete with it? Here the parts shift?
> Here the creature surpass the Creator?—the end, what began?
> Would I in my impotent yearning do all for this man,
> And dare doubt He alone shall not help him, who yet alone can?
>
> . . . . . .
>
> Would I suffer for him that I love? so wouldst Thou—so wilt Thou!
> So shall crown Thee the topmost, ineffablest, uttermost crown,
> And Thy love fill infinitude wholly, nor leave, up nor down,
> One spot for the creature to stand in."

I have no wish to disparage in any way the later poets; I have no doubt that in some ways, and on some subjects, they wrote better poetry than the Hebrews. These words of theirs on the sublimest of topics are very welcome to us, and move us to grateful feelings; but their effect upon us, as compared with that produced by Moses and Asaph and Isaiah, is as moonlight unto sunlight, and as water unto wine.

But to return once more to our direct work. We have now finished with *olam*. We have done with it as we did with *ad*, and have found that it has no more to do with never-endingness, or with duration of any length, than the other word has; and after doing our best to make our work impartial and constructive, we may conclude, without much fear of contradiction, that the true meaning of *olam* has been set forth.

It is a great word. It has nothing to do with imagination and dreams, nor with anything that cannot be verified. It is a word kept for things fixed and certain; a word of observation and insight and, even in its loftiest applications, of experimental proof.

CHAPTER X.

NEW TESTAMENT.

I hope everyone will reject any interpretations of mine which seem to them strained and artificial. The more I read the Bible and believe it, the deeper is my sense of the fearful sin of sacrificing truth in the slightest degree for the sake of making out a case in favour of it. God has confounded many such tricks which have been resorted to in support of His cause. May He confound mine if I have committed what I know must be a more grievous offence in His eyes than many open professions of doubt or unbelief.—MAURICE.

COMING from the Old Testament to the New, we once more find ourselves in front of that saying in the Epistle to the Hebrews which was our starting-point at the first:—

> Thy throne, O God, is for ever and ever.

The value of this text for our purpose is that we know it to be a quotation from the Hebrew psalms, and that there it reads, Thy throne, O God, is *olam ad*—words expressive of Fixity and Prominence always, and never of Duration.

The reader knows also that the Epistle to the Hebrews, though it has come down to us in Greek, was written to and for Hebrews, as, of course, the title of the letter shows. By-and-by we shall study the Greek words as we have studied the Hebrew; but that will be in subsequent chapters. In this the reader will be asked to consider, before, let us say, we know anything whatever about the Greek, how strong and even conclusive is the presumptive proof that For ever and ever is an incorrect translation. Our doing so will involve our looking again at some matters glanced at in the introductory chapter, but the importance of the work in hand will excuse a little repetition.

The writer of the Epistle was probably himself a Hebrew; but if not, if he were a Greek, that would not affect the argument. The point is he was not writing to Greeks, but to Jews; and he was not quoting from Grecian literature, but from Hebrew. Perhaps as he wrote he had the Hebrew Scriptures before him, and himself turned the Hebrew into Greek. Perhaps, as is more likely, he copied from the ancient Greek Version called the Septuagint. This again is a matter which need not give us any concern. The plain fact for us to keep in view is that he or they tried, beyond all question, *to put a Hebrew thought into Greek words.* In this endeavour they either succeeded or they failed; and what verdict we shall have to pronounce remains to be seen when we shall have looked into the Greek. The translators did look into the Greek, and turned it into For ever and ever. Whether they in their turn were right or wrong must also wait until we have made some acquaintance with the Greek.

But it is undeniably certain that somebody has blundered. *Olam ad* never said anything about For ever and ever. The phrase in passing out of Hebrew through Greek into English has fallen among—certain persons who have maltreated it and left it more than half dead; and many have been those who have passed by, just as though it were all right. And such is the force of preconception and custom and conservatism (three terms, one may say, often having much the same meaning), that most people will refuse to believe there can be anything the matter with a phrase so familiar, not to say sacred, as For ever and ever.

The vagueness of the phrase, again, is, according to the views adopted in these pages, and among them the greater regard felt for prophets and apostles than for translators, strongly suggestive of unsoundness in the rendering. It is not seers' language; it is not revelation. If For ever by itself means never-ending duration, what does the bringing in and the adding on to it of a second For ever signify? A scientific treatise, or a business letter, must use language that is precise and informing; but it would seem that words about such matters as the Throne of God and the destiny of men may be the very opposite, and yet be conceived of as Divinely inspired.

And this putting together of presumptive evidence requires me once more to recur to the alternative phrase of the revisers, Unto the ages of the ages, and to say that it is worse than the other. It is as though the translators and revisers had been contenders for ambiguity, and the revisers had won the prize. Because you may interrogate Unto the ages of the ages as much as you please, but for any response of reality to be got from it you will find it as dumb as Baal at Carmel. And the revisers themselves are not altogether satisfied with it. As we saw, they desert it when the reading is in the singular number, and leave For ever and ever unchallenged and untouched. But they could not have been unaware that if the singular number signified Eternity, the plural must have done the same, only, as we might say, more so.

All this seems, in the writing of it, to be too much like fault-finding, but it is necessary for the reader to realize what a strong position he has gained by a little knowledge of things from the Hebrew standpoint. And as for a little hostile criticism, the whole history of For ever and ever is so provocative of raillery and satire, that it is a case of being surprised at one's moderation.

Another indication that there was something in the thought of unending duration, in some of its applications, in connection with the words we are considering, from which the revisers shrank, is found in the fact that they have given up the use of the word Everlasting and replaced it by Eternal. Why they did so is not to be seen very readily. The dictionaries say Eternal generally implies without beginning or end; Everlasting is restricted to that which is without end. Archbishop Whately is of the same opinion. He says:—

Both terms imply endless duration; but Eternal extends to something more—that, viz., which has always existed. Many infidel writers hold that the world is eternal, that is, that it never had a beginning. The heathens believed that their gods were everlasting—*i.e.*, immortal, but not eternal, for their birth and origin were always recorded.

But it is certain this opinion was not entertained by the revisers. They use the word Eternal in translating sayings of Jesus and St. Paul about punishment and destruction; as, for instance:—

Matt. xxv. 26. These shall go away into eternal punishment.

2 *Thess.* i. 9. Who shall suffer punishment, even eternal destruction from the face of the Lord, and from the glory of His might.

Now if Whately's distinction were just, and the revisers had accepted it, they could not have written Eternal punishment and Eternal destruction; for to do so would be to speak, not only of punishment and destruction as being unending, but also as never having had any beginning!

In changing Everlasting into Eternal the revisers must have had in their minds, if not in their intention, some shade of difference of signification, and it is a pity they did not give us some hint of what it was. As it is, there can be no doubt that to many people Whately's statement that Eternal points backward as well as forward is a true account of the customary use of language. Hence the substitution of Eternal only tends to increase the difficulty involved in the application of such a word as Everlasting to *processes*, such as punishment and destruction.

But the attentive listener to human speech cannot but notice there is a use of such words as Eternal in which, strictly speaking, there is no thought either of never beginning or of never ending, This is the case when we say, I will never consent, or when we speak of some very loquacious person as making an eternal chatter. Perhaps a better illustration is a remark attributed to Dr. Adam Clarke. Speaking of a doctrine of Methodist theology prominent in his time, he is reported to have said, Eternal Sonship is eternal nonsense. It seems to me that no one can fail to perceive the two senses given to the word in this brief sentence. Eternal Sonship meant to the speaker Sonship that had no beginning, a Sonship that had been in existence from all eternity. But he could not apply the word to Nonsense with the same meaning, for that would be to say, Sonship that has no beginning is nonsense that has no beginning. The idea which the Doctor really meant to express was, The thought of Sonship without beginning is a fixity of nonsense. And one may say that had the word Eternal been used of Sonship in that same sense of fixity, or certainty, by Clarke's opponents, no objection would have been taken to it.

And as we think of the revisers' change of Everlasting into Eternal, I may venture to suggest that the true idea, Fixity, partly felt but not fully recognized, was controlling such language as the revisers were able to place at its service, and endeavouring after definite expression. That is a way truth has.

But to return to the ordinary meaning of For ever, one of our theological writers, Professor Banks, says it might be enough to ask, as decisive of the question, If this is not the New Testament word for Eternal, what is? He points to the fact that another word taken to have the same meaning only occurs in two passages; and he inquires again if it will be pretended that these are the only New Testament passages in which the idea occurs.

The two texts to which reference is made are these:—

Romans i. 20. His everlasting power and divinity.

Jude 6. Angels which kept not their own principality, but left their proper habitation, He hath kept in everlasting bonds under darkness unto the judgment of the great day.

In the first passage it is doubtful that St. Paul used this other word in the sense of Everlasting. The context seems rather to require the idea that the power and divinity, although invisible, are yet conspicuous through the things that are made. Ewing's Lexicon sees in the word *aidios* a likeness, perhaps more, to our old acquaintance *ad;* and certainly the idea of Prominence seems to be in St. Paul's mind.

Be this as it may, the reader will see for himself that the thought of Never-endingness is not present in the second verse. The angels are kept in "everlasting" bonds, not for ever and ever, at least the text does not say so, but unto the judgment of the great day.

So that if the Greek word with which we shall have to deal in subsequent chapters does not mean Eternal, the presence of the idea in the New Testament is even more rare than was suggested; it may even be doubted whether it can be found at all.

But let us ask, with all earnestness, if it is really necessary that the idea of Eternity should appear in Scripture. To say it is not would seem, I suppose, to many people an attack upon the foundations of the Christian religion; it would to them be subversive of so much, and would suggest such tremendous revolutions in religious thought. But let them not be alarmed. The rock upon which the Church is built is *olam*, and none can injure it.

To say the idea of Eternity must be in Scripture is to assume the right of deciding what ought to be there. And this will look like hoisting oneself with one's own petard; because I have written on the assumption that revelation means bringing a thing into our knowledge, and that to know we must be able to demonstrate. But it strikes me as being a very different thing to say this, and a very reasonable thing to say as compared with saying that things must be in revelation which cannot be known and cannot be verified, except, by inference, in the single case of the nature of the Supreme.

The idea of Eternity is metaphysical, transcendental; it belongs to thought, not to experience. But from a revelation of religion, if one looks at it naturally, and in harmony with its purpose, we expect, not abstractions, but things made prominent, and shown to be certain. This, as we have seen, was eminently the case with the Hebrew seers of the Old Testament; and we must think it is the same with the writers of the New Testament, for they were men of the same race, whose understandings had been opened to the meaning of Moses and the prophets. That it is not so with our English Versions, and that on the most important subject of which we can conceive, cannot but suggest the inference that the makers of them have missed the mark.

The presumptive proof that the For ever and ever interpretation is inaccurate will be as complete as we can make it, if we take what we have learned from the Hebrew words to the examination of passages in which the phrase occurs, and see if they support our theory. If we find we can give a more satisfactory account of them than is done either by For ever and ever, or by Unto the ages of the ages, we may take it that so far our case is made out.

I will quote the first instance from the Revisers' Version :—

Rev. i. 18. I am the first and the last, and the Living One; and I was dead, and behold I am alive for evermore. Gr. *Unto the ages of the ages*.

Everyone must feel that this is a most emphatic statement, and that it is the intention of the speaker to make it so. The way to understand it, then, is to ask what particular fact it is that He wishes to emphasize. And the answer to the question is easily found. If the English is right, it is Christ's eternity that is averred. If the amendment suggested by the revisers is correct, then the stress is on the assertion that He is alive unto the ages of the ages. If our theory is to be preferred, the emphatic truth is that He who was dead is certainly alive; that this is the *certainty of certainties*. I venture to think there can be little hesitation in receiving this as the true drift of the phrase.

One consideration will, I hope, induce the most reluctant reader to accept it gladly. To declare that Jesus is alive for ever and ever is to make a statement which is to be taken on authority, and as a matter of belief only. But to say that His being alive is an *olam*, a fixity, or a certainty, and, indeed, a certainty of certainties, is not only to make a statement; it is, in accordance with Hebrew manner, to challenge test and proof. We cannot know that His being alive is a certainty unless it can be demonstrated; but, according to the preaching and teaching of the apostles, it can be verified. They do not define the life for us; we may not be able to conceive to ourselves how, in what way, He can be alive. But love and trust are not states of mind and feeling to be called into existence and kept in vigour by the dead. And Christianity is based upon the proof of the fact that Jesus, the Son of Love, though crucified, is not killed. It is the forgetting or the ignoring of this, the Church's one foundation, and the putting of other things in its place, that is, as St. Paul and the rest of them tell us, the weakness of the Church; for, really, men are made Christians by the personal verification of the fact that Jesus lives.

It may be said that such a phrase as The certainties of the certainties is not English, any more than that sentence of the revisers to which exception was taken on that very account. Neither is it; nor is it Greek. But it is, or represents, very good Hebrew. When we say King of kings, or the Book of books, we are trying to express the superlative degree as would a Hebrew; only we put the first word in the singular, while he often put it in the plural. Thus he speaks of the heavens of heavens, and of the holies of the holies. This he does because he thinks of heaven as a collection of parts, and so of the holy place. In the latter were the tables, the mercy-seat, and so on; these things were the holies of holies. If we spoke correctly of the Bible we should call it the Books of books rather than the Book of books, because it is really not one book, but a collection of books. In the same way we may think of a Certainty as having parts or divisions. For instance, with regard to the fact of Jesus being alive, we may think of Him as living Teacher, living Priest, and living King, and may say these are the certainties of certainties, our meaning, of course, being that the fact we have in view is a superlative certainty.

But I do not think we can use the words Unto the ages of the ages with the same lucidity, or even with any lucidity at all. True, we may think of the first Ages in the sentence as having parts or divisions; but the second Ages bothers and bewilders us utterly. It is impossible to define them. The structure of the sentence ought to leave us with the thought of the superlative ages. Now, what the superlative certainties are we know; but what the superlative ages may be we do not know, and cannot discover; and if we could we should have no means of verification. Yet the revisers would have us think the Light of the world told the beloved disciple that He was alive unto the superlative ages!

For ever and ever is found most frequently in what are called the Doxologies. There are too many of them for us to examine all, so I will give a specimen from each of three writers:—

Gal. i. 3-5. Grace to you and peace from God the Father, and our Lord Jesus Christ, who gave Himself for our sins, that He might deliver us out of this present evil world, according to the will of our God and Father : to whom be the glory for ever and ever. Amen.

Jude 24, 25. Now unto Him who is able to guard you from stumbling, and to set you before the presence of His glory without blemish in exceeding joy, to the only God our Saviour, through Jesus Christ our Lord, be glory, majesty, dominion, and power, before all time, and now, and for evermore. Amen.

Rev. vii. 11, 12. And all the angels were standing round about the throne, and about the elders and the four living creatures; and they fell before the throne on their faces, and worshipped God, saying, Amen : Blessing, and glory, and wisdom, and thanksgiving, and honour and power, and might, be unto our God for ever and ever. Amen.

Standing for a moment to listen to these Doxologies, they sound to us like the expression of wishes that glory, honour, and power, and so on, may be given to God for ever, or, as the revisers suggest, Unto the ages of the ages. They seem to us desires or prayers for what may be, not statements and declarations of what is. And our use of the word Amen strengthens the impression; for to us Amen means So let it be, as in the prayer, Granting us in this world knowledge of Thy truth, and in the world to come life everlasting. Amen.

But the question is not what it means to us, but what it meant to Bible writers. And Amen is a Hebrew word which means So it is, and not So be it. It is an expression of adherence, or faithfulness, to truth or fact. So God is called the God of the Amen; and Jesus Christ is the Amen, the faithful and true Witness. Thus, if we again look at the Doxologies quoted, we must think that St. Paul followed his, To whom be glory for ever and ever, with an emphatic So it is.

But this creates a difficulty, because the first part, To whom be glory, looks as much like a wish as ever; and how could St. Paul express a desire and in the same breath aver that what he desires is already there?

The answer is that the word To in To Whom represents the sign of the dative case, and should here be replaced by In; and that Be ought to be altered too. There is no verb in the original, and we are left to our common sense to decide whether supplying the verb, as we must do to make sense in English, we should say, In Him *be* glory, so it is; or, In Him *is* glory, so it is. I do not think common sense will hesitate long.

It will help us if we turn to one of the Old Testament Doxologies, which, as we may suppose, the apostles had in their minds when they wrote their own.

1 *Chron.* xxix. 10, 11. Blessed be Thou, O Jehovah, the God of Israel our father, for ever and ever. Thine, O Lord, is the greatness, and the power, and the glory, and the victory, and the majesty.

In the first part of these words of King David our version reads, Blessed *be* Thou, O Jehovah. In the second part it says, Thine *is* the glory. But there is no verb in the original in either place; and common sense, our only guide in such a matter, tells us that David said, Blessed *art* Thou, O Jehovah, as well as, Thine is the greatness.

The whole subject of Blessing and Cursing would, if gone into, show a striking difference between Hebrew religious thought and our own. It must suffice to say that when people bless and curse in the Bible an examination of the words used will point to the fact that they did not, as we do, express a wish that something good or bad might happen; they spake, with emphasis, of a state or condition conceived of as already existing. The Englishman curses emphatically, but not lucidly; and when he says, Bless God, or, God bless you, however energetic his speech may be it is not clear; it implies that he wishes something, but what it is he does not define. The worshipper of the *olam* God could speak with confidence and clearness, and David in the Doxology affirms what *is*: Worthy art thou, O Jehovah, to the certainty of certainties.

I have inserted the words suggested as an improvement on For ever and ever that the reader may judge how they fit. To say Jehovah is worthy for ever is to say more than Jehovah is worthy unto the ages; but I cannot doubt that some such phrase as Jehovah is worthy to a certainty is much more in accordance both with verbal meanings and with the manner of speech about Jehovah customary with Hebrew thinkers.

Returning to the quotations from the New Testament, I think St. Paul said, *In* whom is the glory. He has been speaking of the Lord Jesus Christ giving Himself for our sins that He might deliver us from this present evil world, according to the will of God. A question might arise in the minds of his readers as to whether God our Father is really so good as to will that. Now glory in Bible language is the manifestation, the shining forth, of goodness. Thus when Moses cried, Shew me Thy glory, the answer was, I will make all My goodness pass before thee. And St. Paul, as it seems to me, asserts that the goodness that could conceive and accomplish so great a work is in God: In Him is the glory; this is a certainty of certainties; so it is. This is the positive and confident way of speaking about the Foremost Fixity peculiar to the Hebrew; while to say, To God *be* the glory, is the fashion common to the Englishman.

St. Jude, in the example from his Epistle, is also contemplating a great work of God. It is nothing less than the setting of sinful men faultless and with exceeding joy in the fierce light which beats upon His throne. If we ask what is required on God's part for such a task as this the apostle supplies the answer. The work needs Glory, and of the most exalted, the most majestic order. And there must be Power, dominating Power, stronger than Sin and Death. At the same time the might must be authoritative; it must have warrant, and be seen to be just and right. And these are the qualities that are ascribed to God in the Doxology. So the purport is: God is able to do this, for in Him are Glory, Majesty, Might, and Authority; this is before or above all certainty; it is certain now; and it leads on our thought to all the certainties with which the subject can be associated: It is so.

In the chorus of praise from the Revelation the Divine work spoken of is an accomplished fact. The scene is a marvel of beauty and suggestiveness, demanding a much more extended notice than can be given here. But we may bring for a moment before our eyes the great multitude which no man can number out of every nation, the white robes of righteousness and the palms of victory, and the words, They shall hunger and thirst no more, and God shall wipe away every tear from their eyes. Looking at it all, we see how much was needed in God to bring to pass so glorious a task, and we see the evidence that God possessed what was required. And the more we look the more we shall see that the worshippers are not giving expression to a series of wishes, closing with a Let it be so, but to statement of facts, reaffirmed by a So it is: The Worth, and the Glory, and the Wisdom, and the cause of Thanksgiving, and the Preciousness, and the Power, and the Endurance are in our God to the certainty of certainties. Amen.

Other instances of the occurrence of For ever and ever need not detain us long. One passage, about smoke going up for ever, we have met with previously, and we understand it now to mean, Her smoke goeth up to a certainty. So in two other cases, Worship Him who liveth for ever and ever (Rev. iv. 10), and, They shall reign for ever and ever (Rev. xxii. 5), the life of God, and the reign of the saints, are to the certainty of certainties. But there is one passage it may be well to look at a little more closely as preparatory to tasks awaiting us later on.

Rev. xx. 10. They (the Beast and the false Prophet) shall be tormented day and night for ever and ever.

To think of the Beast and the false Prophet, whoever they may be, tormented without cessation, and to all eternity, is impossible to anyone who comes to the New Testament by way of the Hebrew Scriptures, and in the light of the *olam* Love. For the word Tormented cannot but call to our minds the torture-chamber and the arbitrary infliction of agonizing pain; while For ever and ever cannot but add the unimaginable horror of an everlasting continuance of it.

The text as it stands in English is one more example of the heightened colour given to Bible scenes and sayings of which mention has been made. When the boat in one of the Gospel stories is overtaken by a storm the translators tell us it was *tossed*. It is the same word that here appears as Tormented. Tossing is bad enough for the boat; but for the rich man in the parable, and for the Beast and false Prophet, it must be Torment! It would trouble us to the point of disbelief to be told they are to be tormented for ever; and we should be troubled, on the other hand, if we thought things would always be easy with them. But there is no need for either thought. They will be distressed day and night to a certainty, but for how long we cannot say.

Looking back over this introductory chapter, prefacing our study of the Greek, I think it will be felt that no amount of prejudice or prepossession on my part will account for all it has brought before us. One New Testament writer we have seen turning Hebrew words, the meaning of which we know, into Greek. If the translators or the revisers have correctly represented his Greek by For ever and ever, or Unto the ages of the ages, then the author of the Epistle to the Hebrews—one of the most profound and exact of Biblical writers—blundered, because the Hebrew words he tried to render have nothing to say either about For ever or Ages.

Now high as is the position our respect gives to the learning and the labour of the distinguished men who translated and revised the Bible for us, one would naturally rather find them in error than discover a blunder in such work as that undertaken by the author of the Epistle to Hebrews. I believe translators and revisers would prefer it too. But surveying the renderings they offered us, we found them vague and uncertain; not a bit like the clear and demonstrable teaching of the Hebrew seers. We saw the revisers warning us against the version of the translators, telling us by implication that it was not Greek, and then putting something in its place that was neither English nor Greek. Going a little further into the matter, we found the revisers showing themselves dissatisfied with their own choice; for they carefully keep it out of sight whenever the singular number would require them to write, Unto the age of the age.

Altogether we could not but suspect the success of both the older and later compilers of our English Versions. So, dropping their renderings, we took the *olam* idea to the Doxologies, and the other places where For ever and ever and Unto the ages of the ages had been inserted, and found that not only did it give a better sense, but in all cases the very sense required by the context.

It was necessary that the reader's attention should be occupied with all this, and that he himself should be, if I may say so, fortified with presumptive proof. For no lexicon or any other authority of the kind with which I am acquainted ever gives to the Greek word *aiōn* any other meaning than that of Duration, long or short, as the case may be. Yet we are to prove that, at all events in the New Testament, *aiōn* means the same as *olam*, a word having no connection with Duration whatever; and that in their use of *aiōn* the New Testament writers carried on from the Old Testament to their own Scriptures a thought absolutely essential to the value of both.

CHAPTER XI.

AIŌN.

He that opposes his own judgment against the consent of the times ought to be backed with unanswerable truths; and he that hath truth on his side is a fool, as well as a coward, if he is afraid to own it because of the currency or multitude of other men's opinions.

DE FOE.

AS our business now is to identify the *aiōn* of the New Testament with the *olam* of the Old there is no need to give more than a passing notice to the other Hebrew word, *ad*, and to its usual representative in the later Scriptures. It is possible that in some places, as in the text so often quoted from the Epistle to the Hebrews, there is the intention to speak of a thing as being prominent in itself, as well as certain; but usually, as in the prepositional use of *ad*, the Greek word *eis* is employed to give prominence to the various kinds of Fixity of which it is believed *aiōn* is indicative. Of this a single instance will suffice, and it will be seen how *eis* and the English Unto, which translates it, both fulfil the purpose of a ☞, by means of which we illustrated the work assigned to *ad* in the Hebrew.

John iv. 14. Whosoever drinketh of the water that I shall give him shall not thirst unto a certainty (*eis ton aiōna*).

Turning to *aiōn*, it was remarked at the close of our

last chapter that the dictionaries, and not these alone, all give the word the sense of Duration. This is what the mightiest of them, Liddell and Scott's, has to say:—

"*Aiōn:* a period of existence; one's lifetime, life; an age, generation; one's lot in life; a long space of time, for ever; an era, epoch, period of a dispensation, this present world."

Every one of these definitions, it will be seen, has in it the element of Duration, except the last, and that is a quotation from the New Testament with which we shall make acquaintance later.

It goes without saying that such a work as this great lexicon must be allowed all the weight that belongs to it. It is universally accepted as an authority of the highest class. Indeed, the scholarship and the research of its compilers have been spoken of by accepted judges in such matters as unequalled. And had our investigation commenced with the Greek and the New Testament, instead of with the Hebrew, it would probably have got no farther than this tremendous volume could have taken us in the quotation I have just given.

But, as we ought sometimes to remind ourselves, there is a kind of reverence, found often in connection with more sacred subjects than a dictionary, which is not respect. Properly to *re*spect we ought first of all to, if not *su*spect, at least *in*spect. Unintelligent and unquestioning acceptance God Himself does not ask of man; and men ought not to expect it from each other, for it is not worthy of either party.

One of the many virtues of Liddell and Scott is that to

which a modest claim has been put forth by the present writer. They make no assertion without offering opportunity of proof for their consulter's consideration. Every definition given by them is accompanied by a reference, so that the reader may turn to the word in the midst of its context and judge if it fits. As an instance I will copy out a passage from Plato referred to in the lexicon as an illustration of *ton aiōna* defined as For ever :—

"Wherefore he resolved to have an image of Eternity, which he made when he set in order the heaven moving according to number, while Eternity rested in unity; and this image we call time. For there were no days and nights and months and years before the heaven was created, but when he created the heaven he created them also. They are all parts of time, and the past and future are created species of time, which we unconsciously but wrongly transfer to the eternal essence; for we say indeed he was, he is, he will be, but the truth is 'he is' alone truly expresses him, and that 'was' and 'will be' are only to be spoken of becoming in time, for they are motions, for that which is immovably the same cannot become older or younger by time."*

This is rather intricate and trying to an impatient reader, but let us pause a moment to analyze it. What does the quotation say that *aiōn* is? It gives, when we look into it, a twofold answer to the question.

Aiōn has no past and no future; the only proper way to speak of it is to say it *is*. In other words, *aiōn* does not become older or younger, but is immovably the same. Now, it seems to me that this is scarcely the way in which a philosopher would speak of what is called unending

* *Jowett's Translation: Timaeus*, 37.

duration. At all events, it would not commend itself to the translators aud revisers, and the upholders of their work, who have given us Everlasting and Eternal, and For ever and ever, and Unto the ages of the ages, as equivalents for *aiōn*. But if these men of erudition, and if Plato himself, had wished to speak of what a Hebrew would think of as an absolute Fixity, in contrast to time, Plato's words would appear to be well chosen.

Again, in the quotation, although time is put in contrast with the *aiōn* of which Plato speaks, it is at the same time said to be an image of it. Now time can hardly be thought of as an image of unending duration. But if we think of the ordered motions of the heavens, sun, moon, and stars, upon which the divisions of time are based, we shall have no difficulty in seeing what the likeness spoken of by Plato really is. They are Fixities; *olams*, as a Hebrew would say. So Plato, so far as I can judge, seems to speak of them as *aiōns;* they are many in number, they move, and are finite, still they are *aiōns;* and, in their relative certainty, images or symbols of the one and absolute Fixity beyond.

To this illustration from Plato I will add one from Aristotle, given in Ewing's dictionary:—

"For the consummation which contains the time of every life that has nothing supernatural is called its *aiōn*. By parity of reason, the consummation of the whole heaven, and the consummation which contains the unbounded duration, and the immensity of all, having taken its name from ever-enduring, is *aiōn*—immortal and divine."*

* *Aristotle on Heaven*, Book I. chap. x.

Here two *aiōns* are mentioned, and a likeness between them is drawn out. The second *aiōn* is so called for the same reason as the first *aiōn* is so called. The first *aiōn* is not Time, but the consummation, or completeness, which contains the time of every life; and the second *aiōn* is not Eternity, though it is ever-during, or always, it is the completeness that contains the unbounded duration and the immensity of all. To put it in another way, *aiōn* is something more than the life-time or age, and something more than eternity, or the ages of the ages; in the one case it is the fixed state, or condition, which includes the life, and in the other it is the fixed order of things, which includes unbounded duration and the immensity of all.

Plato and Aristotle lived somewhere about the time when the translation of the Hebrew Scriptures into Greek was undertaken by the learned Jews, whose work is called the Septuagint. They would have to search for and choose a word which would express in Greek what *olam* meant in Hebrew. Their work conclusively shows that they fixed upon *aiōn* as suited for their purpose; and the quotations from Plato and Aristotle, two masters in Greek literature, seem to afford independent indication that *aiōn*, capable, like *olam*, of application to limited and to absolute fixity, was the very word they needed.

After this we do not stand in so much awe of the lexicons as we otherwise might. And as to other authoritative utterances which tell us the primary meaning of *aiōn* is Duration, and that of its adjective *aiōnios* Eternal, Bishop Westcott will hearten us very considerably. In commenting upon St. John's Epistles he says :—

"In considering these phrases it is necessary to premise that in spiritual things we must guard against all conclusions which rest upon the notions of duration and succession. 'Eternal life' is that which St. Paul speaks of as the life which is life indeed. It is not an endless duration of being in time, but being of which time is not a measure."

Yet the Revised Version renders *ton aiōna* many times by For ever, and *aiōnios* always by Eternal. And Bishop Westcott was one of the Revision Company. It is an advantage to be able to appeal from a reviser as one of a company to a reviser in his individual capacity. No doubt he was an advocate for some better phrase than For ever and ever, or Unto the ages of the ages, and was outvoted. For matters of this kind were settled by vote, like another penny added to the income tax, as, indeed, were great doctrines in ancient times; and votes were not weighed; and they were, and it is not uncharitable to say so, sometimes influenced by other motives than exclusive regard to the matter in hand.

Giving attention now to our own proper business, but from which we have not really been diverted by these only apparently digressive excursions, I will quote two or three texts in further proof of the fact that *aiōn* was chosen or adopted by New Testament writers as the representative and successor of *olam*.

    1 *Peter* i. 25. All flesh is as grass,
                        And all the glory thereof as the flower of grass.
                        The grass withereth, and the flower falleth:
                        But the word of the Lord abideth *eis ton aiōna*.

The English Version says For ever, and of the word of God that is of course true. But it is true only as a secondary, or consequent, and not as the primary meaning. The text is quoted from Isaiah's great chapter about the *olam* God. God's word, like Himself, is inviolate to all destructive influences. Like Love, it is a flower that does not fall. This is what Isaiah expressed by *olam;* and St. Peter, wanting to put the prophet's thought into Greek, accepted *aiōn* as a competent medium.

In this case we cannot complain of For ever as hiding from us much of the writer's meaning, though it does a little; but in the next instance the loss is serious:—

Heb. v. 6. Thou art a priest *eis ton aiōna* (For ever) after the order of Melchisedec.

Mr. Stead says people in these days do not want to hear anything about Melchisedec. Perhaps they do not. But he will agree they need to know a good deal about Jesus Christ, and that they cannot know Him as the writers of the New Testament knew Him without some comprehension of the great argument based by the author of the Epistle to Hebrews upon the quotation I have given. That argument is briefly as follows:—

The account of Melchisedec given in the Book of Genesis is taken as a symbol or illustration of Jesus Christ as Priest. Two things are particularly noticed. One of these is the *greatness* of Melchisedec. He is King of Righteousness and King of Peace, he blesses Abraham, the father of the Hebrew race, and receives tithes of him; and through Abraham the Mosaic priesthood itself may be said to have acknowledged the superiority of Melchisedec by paying tithes to him. The other point is this: Seeing no sign is given of the origin of Melchisedec, of father, mother, or genealogy, and no hint is found of the ending of his life, he may be said, for purposes of illustration, to abide a priest *perpetually*.

It is in these that the "order" of Melchisedec consists; and as Christ is a Priest after the order of Melchisedec it is, of course, in these that His likeness to Melchisedec is to be found. But more especially is this the case with regard to the perpetuity of His Priesthood, for this, as we shall see, really involves the greatness of it.

This idea of perpetuity or continuity is set forth in the following passages:—

Heb. vii. 16. Who hath been made, not after the law of a carnal commandment, but after the power of an endless life.

Heb. vii. 25. He ever liveth to make intercession for them.

Heb. x. 12. But He, when He had offered one sacrifice for sins for ever sat down on the right hand of God.

Heb. x. 14. For by one offering He hath perfected for ever them that are sanctified.

Now it is particularly to be noticed that although the idea of perpetuity or everlastingness occurs in all four of these sayings, not one of them contains *aiōn*, or any word related to it. But, and this for our object is most important of all, the idea of continuance in the quotations is based upon and results from the *aiōns* that are found in other places. Here they are:—

Heb. vii. 24. He, because He abideth [or, because of the abiding of Him], *eis ton aiōna*, hath His priesthood unchangeable (or intransmissible).

Heb. vii. 28. For the law appointed men high priests having infirmity; but the word of the oath, which was after the law, a Son, *eis ton aiōna* perfected.

Can there be a doubt that the author of the Epistle, writing to Hebrew people, had his mind full of the thought of *olam*? And to him on such a subject *olam* must have had its full sense of absolute inviolability. The Jewish priests were hindered by death from continuing. Death has wrought its utmost upon Jesus, but He still abides. And because He is *olam*, He ever liveth to make intercession.

And not only is He inviolate as regards death, but as regards "infirmity," which was another characteristic of the Jewish priesthood. Jesus is perfected, or complete, *eis ton aiōna;* His completeness is *olam*.

This thought is a pregnant one to the author of the Epistle, as well it might be, and he dwells upon it at length. It may be said, indeed, to underlie the whole of his reasoning. The priests of the Mosaic order were not always true to God; Jesus is faithful in all God's house. They at times were not sympathetic; He is made in all things like unto His brethren. The old Temple was a shadow, the sacrifices could not take away sin, the ancient covenant was broken; Christ has entered the true tabernacle, He saves to the uttermost, and His covenant is inviolate. The Jewish priests stand day by day ministering and offering sacrifices which can never take away sin, always striving after that which can never be accomplished; He, when he had offered His sacrifice, cried, It is finished, and for ever sat down on the throne of God.

Thus *aiōn* is *olam*. It is a greater word than For ever. In this case it is, as Aristotle might have said, the *aiōn* "immortal and divine, which contains" not only the indissoluble life, but also that absolute perfection of priesthood by which we draw nigh to God, and which will draw all men unto itself.

Another link uniting the Old Testament and the New is found in a saying of St. Paul :—

1 *Tim.* i. 17. The King eternal, immortal, invisible, the only God.

The English Version turns a noun into an adjective, and the margin of the Revised Version suggests as a correction, King of the Ages. St. Paul wrote, King of the *aiōns*, and, after what has been said, the expression will be found clear and forceful and exceedingly suggestive. And it is just in the Hebrew method.

In one of the psalms it is said :—

Psalm cxlv. 13. Thy kingdom is an everlasting kingdom.

This in the original is, Thy kingdom is a kingdom of all *olams*, and the reader, knowing that, will probably feel sure that St. Paul, a Hebrew of Hebrews, had some such thought in his mind when he wrote, The King of the *aiōns*.

The kingdom of the Christ will doubtless be everlasting. We are told so in the following words, though not exactly in the way that a casual glance at them would recognize :—

Luke i. 33. The Lord God shall give unto Him the throne of His father David; and He shall reign over the house of Jacob *eis tous aiōnas* (for ever); and of His kingdom there shall be no end.

This is one of the instances where, the Greek being in the plural, the revisers put Unto the ages in their margin; why they do so they do not say, and nobody else knows. If the singular means For ever, the plural ought to mean For evers!

The speaker of the words, though an angel, was thinking in Hebrew fashion of the Fixity in his mind, and which he had come to announce, as a whole, having parts. Uttering such a prediction as he does about an unborn Child, we can see that it is not unnatural that he should so speak, albeit we are not accustomed to look at things in the Hebrew way. The Child must be born, and it must be a Boy; the Boy must live and grow, and the Man must be good and wise; and He must gain that ascendancy over the house of Jacob without which He could not reign. Every way the prospect suggested doubts, and Gabriel's words cover them all: He shall reign to the certainties.

Then another thought is brought in, Of His kingdom there shall be no end. If he had already said, He shall reign for ever, this would be tautological and redundant; and it is not respectful to divine messengers to represent them as talking in that way.

St. John does not appear to have quoted any Old Testament passage having *olam* in it, but his use of the Greek is not less clear than that of the other writers quoted. Perhaps no part of the New Testament has suffered so much as have his Gospel and his Letters from this fact having been obscured. The following text is an instance:—

1 *John* ii. 17. The world passeth away, and the lust thereof; but he that doeth the will of God abideth for ever.

When some thoughtful person reads this, or hears it read, he cannot but ask himself, Does the apostle really mean what he says? The world is not passing away. We found it here when we arrived, and we shall leave it here when we depart. And he that doeth the will of God does not abide for ever, he vanishes from the scene. This is the kind of thing that makes the Bible a disturbance to some minds, and worse than that to others.

St. John does not say the world is passing away, or that it is doing anything else; he speaks in the passive voice, and says something is being done to the world—its veil is being stripped off, it is losing its disguise, and its desire of the flesh, its desire of the eyes, and its vain glory of life, are being shown to be the falsities they really are. In other words, the shining of the true light, the advent of worthier knowledge, shows the untruth and insufficiency of the world, as men have made it, and as a consequence the lust or desire of it.

But that same light shining on the doer of God's will takes nothing from him; he abideth inviolate.

Pausing for a moment at this stage to look back, and then forward to what has still to be done, we may take it for granted that *aiōn* in the New Testament, like *olam* in the Old, will always speak to us of some kind or form of Fixity. As against the dictionaries and the versions, we have the evidence of the author of the Epistle to Hebrews, Plato and Aristotle, Bishop Westcott, St. Peter, St. Paul, the angel Gabriel, and St. John. In such company, or, rather, with such supporters, we need not be abashed.

What we have to do now is to point out the various kinds of Fixity *aiōn* is employed to speak of. There will have to be some sort of interlude to afford us an opportunity of saying something about the famous fight over the words World and Age as interpreters of *aiōn*, but it will hardly be a digression. All the remaining texts in the New Testament not previously quoted, in which *aiōn* is rendered by For ever, may be included under the idea of *Fixity of Fact*, and to this we will now address ourselves. The result of inquiry, I venture to think, will not be disappointing even in the case of texts familiar and endeared.

Take, for instance :—

John vi. 58. I am the living bread which came down from heaven: if any man eat of this bread he shall live *eis ton aiōna*.

Anyone can see how absurd it would be here to make use of the phrase kept for use by the revisers when the number is plural, and read, He shall live unto the age. But For ever is open to another kind of objection. To tell a man he shall live for ever if he will eat the bread of life, is to tell him what he cannot begin to verify until after he has died. To say he shall certainly live, and giving the word its full force as the nature of the case requires, and live violably, or be invulnerable to all the ills which tend to make life not worth the living, is not only to offer him a great and present boon, it is also to offer him something whose reality he can at once proceed to test. The fixity set forth is a fixity of Fact.

So with the following :—

Mark xi. 14. And He answered and said unto it, No man eat fruit from thee henceforward *eis ton aiōna*.

Jude 13. Wandering stars, for whom the blackness of darkness hath been reserved *eis ton aiōna*.

It was a fact that no man should again eat fruit of the fig tree. And the wandering stars may be bright enough as they pursue their erratic course; but it is a fixed thing that the blackness of darkness hath been reserved for them.

Whether they will emerge from that darkness or not, *aiōn* says absolutely nothing, either on the one side or the other.

The same kind of Fixity is denoted when *aiōn* is accompanied by a negative, and appears in the English Version in the form of Never:—

Mark iii. 29. Whosoever shall blaspheme against the Holy Ghost hath never forgiveness, but is in danger of eternal damnation.

John viii. 51. If a man keep My saying he shall never see death.

John x. 28. They shall never perish, neither shall any man pluck them out of My hand.

John xiii. 8. Peter saith unto Him, Thou shalt never wash my feet.

The reader will remember a text in the Old Testament, The sword shall never depart from thy house, where, from the construction of the original, we felt constrained to read, The sword shall not depart from thy house up to the point of fixity, or, Thy house shall not be able to count upon freedom from the sword as a certainty. If the translators had put the passages just cited as, Thou shalt not wash my feet for ever, and, They shall not perish for ever, there would have been some ambiguity in the rendering. We may have thought Peter to mean the Master might wash his feet, but not for ever; and that Jesus inferred His sheep might perish, but not eternally. So it is with our own form of words. Hath not forgiveness to a certainty might be, Certainly had not forgiveness, or, Hath not forgiveness up to the point of being sure about it.

All this may be thought trivial, but in reality a great deal depends upon our being able to read some of these texts with exactness. The Burial Service says, Whosoever liveth and believeth in Him shall not die eternally. And that is just as though we read the text to which it refers as, He that liveth and believeth on Me shall not die for ever, or, Shall not die to a fixity.

Peter's saying seems to keep us right. He could not mean, Thou shalt not wash my feet eternally; his intention was, Thou shalt certainly not wash my feet. And so we must understand the sheep of Christ are, in His words, certainly not to perish. While the Burial Service, conveying as it does the inference that those who do not believe will die for ever, and that those who do may die for a time, misquotes with dire effect the great saying of Jesus, He that liveth and believeth in Me shall certainly not die. It is a fixity of fact.

The text about blaspheming the Holy Ghost will exercise us a good deal before we finish. Just now it will suffice to notice the precise sense of *aiōn*. The words, Hath never forgiveness, but is in danger of eternal damnation, look rather contradictory. If a man *never* has forgiveness he would seem to be sure, and not merely in danger, of eternal damnation. But passing by this for the present, the first part of the quotation appears undoubtedly to have the sense of, Hath certainly not forgiveness. Whether the fixity in this case be absolute or not must be decided on other grounds.

A look at three other texts will complete this stage of our inquiry:—

Heb. xiii. 8. Jesus Christ the same yesterday, and to-day, and for ever.

John xiv. 16. I will pray the Father and He shall give you another Comforter, that He may be with you for ever, even the Spirit of truth: whom the world cannot receive.

John viii. 35. The servant abideth not in the house for ever: the Son abideth for ever.

As we read these verses the writers seem at first to be speaking of Duration, and, especially in the last two, to be drawing a contrast between shorter and longer duration. But a little attention will show they are really calling our notice to matters of fact.

In the first the author of the words is endeavouring after steadfastness and faithfulness on the part of those to whom he writes. As an incentive, he says, Jesus Christ (is) yesterday and to-day the same, even to the certainties—all the certainties, or parts of the fixity, that can be thought of in the case. And his next words are, Be not carried away by divers and strange teachings.

In the second the contrast is not between the departing Christ and the abiding Spirit, but between the disciples who shall possess the Spirit to a certainty and the world which cannot receive the Spirit, because it beholdeth Him not neither knoweth Him. The possession of that great help, the Spirit of truth or fact, is for the followers of the Christ a fixity of fact.

And the contrast in the last of the three passages is not what we may probably be led by the English reading to think it is. Jesus could not speak of the slave, and that a slave of sin, and the Son as both being of the house; and with no other distinction between them than that the one is of it temporarily and the other perpetually. If we have read correctly in other places we must understand Jesus to say here, The slave certainly abideth not in the house; on the other hand, it is a fact that the Son does so abide. And the contrast is not between one who is of the house for ever and one who is only of it for a time, but between Him who, to a certainty, is a Son of the house and the slave who is not of the house at all. The whole argument, which is a little obscured perhaps by compression, is apparently, You say you are of the house because you are Abraham's seed; but if you sin you are slaves, and slaves are certainly not of the house. The Son is as certainly an abider in the house; if, therefore, the Son shall make you free of the house you will be free indeed.

This seems to complete the texts, or classes of texts, in which *aiōn* is rendered by For ever, and, at the same time, those in which it really seems to speak of a fixity of fact. There are other fixities, but these will come in another chapter.

CHAPTER XII.

AIŌN AS WORLD AND AGE.

> Mankind in general are so little in the habit of looking steadily at their own meaning, or of weighing the words by which they express it, that the writer who is careful to do both (as is the case with the Bible writers) will sometimes mislead his readers through the very excellence which qualifies him to be their instructor.—COLERIDGE.

BEFORE proceeding to indicate and set forth in order the instances of other kinds of Fixity to which *aiōn* points it is necessary to speak at some length of the translators' and revisers' choice and use of the words World and Age as equivalent in meaning to the Greek word. And although it may be deemed invidious, or worse, to offer evidence of their indecision in the use of these terms and of the inability of the words themselves to do what is required of them, the gain to our own theory seems to be so great that the temptation is not to be withstood.

It goes without saying that the makers of the Authorized Version could not maintain their notion of For ever in all cases of *aiōn's* appearance. Take such texts as the following in illustration of this:—

Matt. xiii. 39. The harvest is the end of the *aiōn*.

2 *Tim.* iv. 9. Demas forsook me, having loved this present *aiōn*.

They could not say, The harvest is the end of the Ever, and so forth, and retain a reputation for sanity; so they

AIŌN AS WORLD AND AGE.   155

bring in a new word, and write, The harvest is the end of the world.

The revisers in their work show their dissatisfaction with the choice of their predecessors. And well they might, for the great Lexicon upon the revisers' table gave not one single reference to such a use of *aiōn* in the classical Greek literature. Thus when they come to the texts about the Harvest and Demas they put in their margin, *Greek:* Age. In this they are in complete accord with the Lexicon; but their agreement with the New Testament writers may be doubted.

Just now the reader is asked to make a note of the fact that the favourite word of King James' company is World, and that it is used by them in almost all cases in which *aiōn* is found without a preposition in front of it. To put it clearly, *eis ton aiōna* means, according to the translators, For ever; but take away the preposition, and the meaning is, The World. And the righteousness, or rightwiseness, of this use has to be tested.

Some time ago we had to ask whether an alteration in number could cause an alteration in nature. The question was suggested by the action of the revisers in rendering *aiōn* in the singular by For ever, and the same word in the plural by Unto the Ages. Now the question arises, Can the presence or absence of a preposition, meaning Unto, make such a difference as that between World and Perpetuity?

The reader will feel impelled to say this is quite incredible, and impossible in any language, except, alas! in that of the English Bible. And he will feel that to say, The harvest is the end of the world, is to be as far from the truth as it would be to attribute to Jesus a saying like, He that liveth and believeth in Me shall not die unto the world! And this we may take as one of the witnesses that World, as an interpreter of *aiōn*, is, notwithstanding the empire accorded it, a great unrecognized incapacity.

Another evidence is found in the fact of the translators being obliged in some cases to acknowledge its uselessness, and, fond as they are of it, to put it under the table out of sight, bringing forward some other word to take its place. The following instances will show this:—

Eph. ii. 7. That in the *aiōns* to come He might show the exceeding riches of His grace.
Col. i. 26. The mystery which hath been hid from all *aiōns*.
Eph. ii. 2. Wherein aforetime ye walked according to the *aiōn* of this world.

In the first two texts they give us Ages instead of Worlds; and in the third they put neither Age nor World, but Course.

Any reader can figure to himself the impossibility of employing World in these cases as is done by the translators in all other instances of the appearance of *aiōn* without a preposition. In the first text, from Ephesians, St. Paul is writing to some of those to whom the riches of grace had been shown; and to make him speak of the grace as being for worlds yet to come would have been manifestly incorrect. And in the quotation from Colossians it would be absolutely false to talk of a mystery, such a "mystery" as the apostle is writing of, as hidden from *all* worlds. The second example in the list from the Epistle to Ephesians is crucial, and most conclusive. If the translators had printed, Wherein aforetime ye walked according to the world of this world, their readers would have thought—what *would* they have thought?

Yet, notwithstanding these weighty testimonials against the competency of their favourite word, the translators cling to it and use it in all cases except these three instances. And, let it be remarked, it is to this, and this alone, that we owe such deeply-cut sentences as The end of the world, and World without end. It may not be possible for long enough yet to convince people that such expressions, if not the religious ideas connected with them, have no other basis than the incorrect rendering of a Greek word; such, nevertheless, appears to be the truth.

When the company of revisers came together to repair and perfect the work of the translators, they had, in having Liddell and Scott's great Lexicon on the table, an advantage not enjoyed by their predecessors. Perhaps it was owing to this fact that Age, as being more of a duration word than World, became their chosen servant. If the reader will look through a copy of the Revised Version he will see that everywhere almost Age is substituted for World, either in the text or in the margin. Demas forsook St. Paul, having loved the present age; a statement very confusing to people who, in the language of one of their hymns, think to fulfil their calling by serving the present age.

Turning to that text in Ephesians about walking according to the *aiōn* of this world, we find Age standing in the margin as the revisers' warning signal that we are not to accept World as a correct account of St. Paul's meaning. Let us then see what we can make of Wherein aforetime ye walked according to the age of this world. As we all know, Age is a flexible term in ordinary English, and we are set thinking, only some people will say we are trifling again, whether the apostle means the world's length of duration, or its stone age, its age of iron, or its golden age.

But a scrutiny of the revisers' use of Age will show they always use it in a rigid sense. To them it never means anything else than Period of duration. So if we accept their suggestion in connection with the text under consideration we must read St. Paul as saying, Wherein aforetime ye walked according to the period of duration of this world!

And here we may see how words, like men and dictionaries, may be accepted as competent and worthy until their fitness is inquired into from the point of view of success in what they profess to accomplish. The King of the Ages has a taking sound, so has He shall reign unto the Ages; but when we see the phrases mean nothing more definite than King of the periods of duration, or He shall reign unto the periods of duration, we are bound to say such language is not, to a certainty, the informing voice of revelation. It is much more like what one might speak of as the jargon of lexical intoxication.

Thus we have the same kind of proof that Age does not bring out the true thought of *aiōn* as that which we applied in the case of World. In the text so often quoted, Wherein aforetime ye walked according to the *aiōn* of this world, Age stands in the margin as a suggested, and

AIŌN AS WORLD AND AGE. 159

supposed preferable, alternative for the word chosen by the translators. But when we take it and read, Ye walked according to the age of this world, it does not enlighten us, and we know it to be a mere pretender.

And as·it was with the translators and their word, so it is with the revisers and theirs; they acknowledge it to be incompetent. When they come upon such passages as those I am about to cite, they give no sign of preference for their own word, and no hint that there is anything amiss with the translation.

Luke i. 70. As He spake by the mouth of His holy prophets, which have been since the *aiōn* (world) began.

John ix. 32. Since the *aiōn* (world) began it was never heard that anyone opened the eyes of a man born blind.

Knowing, as we do know, the hold, strong and tyrannous, which Age had upon the revisers, as shown by the fact that they have in practically all cases, except those just adduced, been impelled to dethrone World in its favour, we may be sure that it was not without a wrench that in these instances they broke away, and allowed World to stand unchallenged. But what else could they do? They could not make Zacharias and the blind man say, Since the Age, or since the period of duration, began. People would have wanted to know what age, or period of duration, was referred to; and there would be none to regard, nor any to answer. Seeing this, there was nothing to be done, in the opinion of the Revision Company, except for the time being to forsake Age and pay homage to World.

And this is what, in the famous scene on Mount Carmel,

was called halting between two opinions. The words do not quite mean the people of Israel were hesitating which god they should serve. They charge them rather with serving both; or, more exactly, with passing from one to the other, not with confidence, but in lame, limp, *halting*, hesitating fashion, as though they were sure of neither. And the way in which the revisers pass from World to Age and back again is, to us, a plain token that they are not certain and wholehearted in their acceptance of either word as a competent interpreter of *aiōn*.

But, it will be asked, is World after all the better word? and is it to be allowed to stand in those sayings of Zacharias and the blind man? As we read those sayings in our English Bible the position of World seems strong and impregnable; so much so, that we can think of no other word, except, perhaps, Time, that would have a chance in contest for its place. Consequently we might tremble for the truth of our own theory that *aiōn* in every place represents some kind of Fixity, were it not that the defences of World in the quotations are altogether shadowy and delusive.

In the words of Zacharias there is nothing about Since and Began. What he said was simply, From *aiōn*. If World be the correct word to use for *aiōn*, then Zacharias should have been reported as saying, Holy From-the-World Prophets; if Age is better, the revisers should have put in the margin, *Greek:* From the age. But it was seen this would not make sense; and two other words, quite unrepresented in the original, are forced in that World may keep its reputation. The revisers were obliged to leave it untouched, for to alter it to Since the age began

AIŌN AS WORLD AND AGE.

would have set people asking that before-mentioned and unanswerable question, What age? It is unquestionably the case that neither World nor Age will fit this passage. But is it the same with the idea of Fixity? The father of John the Baptist is speaking of the Salvation of God testified to by the prophets. His endeavour, as the whole context shows, is to impress his hearers with the *certainty* of prophetic speech on this topic. The prophets were Holy; they were more than Holy, they were, and spake, from Certainty. It was an *olam* matter to this Israelite, who stands, so to say, betwixt the Old and New Testaments; and for myself I cannot see how his use of *aiōn* can be taken in any other sense.

And the blind, or once blind, young man, who so sturdily championed Jesus against the Pharisees, did not say, Since the world began. The words Since and Began have been put in to make sense of World. What he did say was, Out of *aiōn*, or Of *aiōn*. Put in that way, the reader can see how the words have been mistranslated, and why. It would not have done for the translators to have printed, Out of the world was it not heard that any man opened the eyes of one born blind. Just as little was it possible that the revisers should say, Such a thing had not been heard of Out of the Age. Of the Age, or of the World, was it not heard, etc., would not have mended matters. Holding their view of the meaning of *aiōn*, there was nothing the translators could do except to introduce other words, for whose presence in the text there is no warrant; and when the revisers came, wishful to put Age in the place of World, but finding it impossible, there seemed nothing possible to them but to wink at the interpolations and pass on.

But it seems perfectly plain that in this place also, where both World and Age are confessedly incapable, the idea of Certainty is the true interpretation. The speaker wishes to assert that it was an unknown thing that a man should open the eyes of one who was born blind. And without imposing a meaning upon words they cannot bear, or adding words of our own to the man's speech to make it say what we think it ought to say, we may understand him as declaring, Of a certainty such a thing as this was never before heard of.

His words speak of a fixity of Fact, as those of Zacharias referred to a fixity of Truth. And going on now with the work of defining and setting in order the various kinds of Fixity alluded to by the use of *aiōn* in the New Testament, we may first of all mention one or two instances which are solitary in their occurrence, or almost solitary. One of these is:—

Hebrews i. 2. By whom also He made the *aiōns*.

Here the reference is, no doubt, to such *olams* as the universe, its motions, and its laws; but not to these alone. The author of the saying had just written, Whom He hath appointed Heir of all things; and in penning the words, By whom also He made the *aiōns*, he has probably in his mind all the fixities of truth and law and nature, and grace, of which we can think, as well as the fixity of a universal inheritance.

In St. Paul's saying—

Col. i. 26. The mystery which hath been hid from all *aiōns*,

AIŌN AS WORLD AND AGE. 163

the word points to a different kind of fixity altogether. It was not a God-made fixity; it was not such as included the voices of the Hebrew seers, for the mystery of which the apostle speaks was not hidden from them. The people to whom he was writing would know well that he referred to the systems of philosophy which, though really opposed to truth, were yet vaunted as solutions and remedies for the perplexities and ills of men, and by their advocates proclaimed as *olams* indeed. The divine mystery was not made known to them.

And yet another kind of fixity is found in the words quoted from the parable of the tares :—

Matt. xiii. 39. The harvest is the consummation of the *aiōn*.

This is a fixed order of things in which good and evil are growing together, and inextricably so. It is beyond the power of man to separate them. Whenever he tries to do so he uproots good as well as evil, as, for instance, in his acts of persecution. And there is no need for him to try. The good will ripen into fruit, the evil into worthlessness; that will be accepted, this rejected. All this is fixity, and the harvest is the consummation of the *aiōn*.

Besides these exceptional fixities, all the others—yet to be noticed—may be classed in three divisions. In the minds, and sometimes in the words, of Jesus and His apostles there was a Fixity which was conceived of as passing away and about to vanish. And in opposition or contrast to this there was a Fixity spoken of as coming. Then there was a third Fixity, which owed whatever it possessed of a fixed character to human opinion and custom and observance. Unless I am mistaken, every passage in which *aiōn* without a preposition is found, except those already quoted, may be put under one or other of these heads.

An example of the first division occurs in a question put to Jesus by His disciples during the last days of His life:—

Matt. xxiv. 3. Tell us, when shall these things be? and what shall be the sign of Thy presence, and of the end of the *aiōn*?

As the question was asked they were looking at the Temple; and Jesus had declared that of its stones not one should be left on another. The Temple represented a fixed order of things which was now coming to an end; and the disciples ask what the sign will be, not of the ending of the world—that is a notion altogether imported by the translators—but of the ending of this ancient and once most sacred Fixity. This interpretation is supported not only by the analogy of other occurrences of *aiōn*, but by the words, Verily I say unto you, this generation shall not pass away until all these things be accomplished Under the supposition that Jesus was speaking of the "end of the world," these words have been subjected to all sorts of torture in order to force them to agree with what has gone before.

There are two other sayings about the same vanishing fixity. One of them is by St. Paul:—

1 *Cor.* x. 11. Now these things happened unto them by way of example; and they were written for our admonition, upon whom the ends of the *aiōns* are come.

The theme is the need for personal effort; privileges are not sufficient. Men had these under the Mosaic order;

they were baptized, and they ate spiritual meat, and drank from the rock, which was Christ. Yet they were overthrown in the wilderness. Now the old order was yielding place to new; God was to fulfil Himself in another way. The end of the ancient fixity had come upon those to whom the apostle was writing. But the point to be borne in mind was that under the new the same rule would prevail; privileges without personal effort would not suffice: Wherefore let him that thinketh he standeth take heed lest he fall.

The other example is from the Epistle to Hebrews :—

Heb. ix. 26. Once at the end of the *aiōns* hath He been manifested to put away sin by the sacrifice of Himself.

If it were worth while we might linger here, as we might have done with the previous quotation, to show how utterly futile it would be to think of World or Age as competent to give us the significance of *aiōn* in such cases as these. But, turning to the context, one of the greatest things in Scripture, we see clearly that the *aiōns* are the fixities of the Jewish priesthood—the sacrifice, the covenant, the temple, and the ministry. In the ending of these, when they are found to be outworn and effete, a new order appears—an *olam* Priest, inviolate and indefectible, an effectual sacrifice, a better covenant enacted upon better promises.

Of the second class of passages, those dealing with a coming fixity, the instances are more numerous. It will be interesting and of service if I put them together in order.

Matt. xii. 32. It shall not be forgiven him, neither in this *aiōn*, nor in that which is to come.

Luke xviii. 30. There is no man that hath left house, or wife, or brethren, or parents, or children, for the kingdom of God's sake, who shall not receive manifold more in this time, and in the *aiōn* to come eternal life.

Luke xx. 35. They that are accounted worthy to attain to that *aiōn*, and the resurrection from the dead, neither marry, nor are given in marriage.

Heb. vi. 5. And tasted the good word of God, and the powers of the *aiōn* to come.

As to these texts, the question arises, Do they refer to some future state of existence or to the present? There can be little doubt what the answer in one case will be. The mention of the resurrection of the dead at once puts our thought beyond the grave, and engages it with a fixed order of things there. But this does not oblige us to look upon *aiōn* as a word to be interpreted, even in this instance, by either World or Age. The words of Jesus speak of a fixed condition, one of the characteristics of which is that people do not marry.

Subversive of popular notions as such a statement may be, it is doubtful if any other text in the list points, at all events exclusively, to anything beyond the life that now is. The sin spoken of in one of them has no forgiveness under the new order, any more than it had under that which, as Jesus spake, was passing away. To give up anything for the kingdom of God's sake is to receive manifold more in the present time, the time of transition, in which the sacrifice is made, and in the coming fixity itself, eternal life. For though we may think, as well as trust, that what our version calls Eternal Life will be ours in future worlds, I hope to be able to show that it is demonstrably something to be attained here. And, to glance at the last passage in the group referring to the coming *aiōn*, men "taste the powers" of it when they are "enlightened and taste of the heavenly gift, and are made partakers of the Holy Spirit."

Finally, there is a third Fixity, one that is not so really, and in truth not absolutely, but made what it is by the thought and custom of man. The passages in which *aiōn* is used in this sense become so lucid once we see the true drift of the word, that I shall need to do little more than quote them. It was this fixity which Demas loved, and for the sake of which he forsook St. Paul, although probably the same counsel had been given him about it as the apostle gave to the Roman Christians:—

Romans xii. 2. Be not fashioned according to this *aiōn*: but be ye transformed by the renewing of your minds.

It has its wisdom, as is recorded by Jesus as well as by St. Paul. The latter does not think much of it, and, indeed, advises anyone who thinks he possesses it to improve himself by becoming a fool.

Luke xvi. 8. The children of this *aiōn* are in their generation wiser than the children of light.

1 *Cor.* ii. 6-8. We speak wisdom among the perfect: yet a wisdom not of this *aiōn*, nor of the rulers of this *aiōn* which are coming to nought: but we speak God's wisdom in a mystery, even the wisdom which hath been hidden, which God foreordained before the *aiōns* unto our glory: which none of the rulers of this *aiōn* knoweth.

1 *Cor.* iii. 18. If any man thinketh that he is wise among you in this *aiōn* let him become a fool, that he may become wise.

According to St. Paul, too, this *aiōn* has its god and its wealth :—

2 *Cor.* iv. 4. In whom the god of this *aiōn* hath blinded the minds of the unbelieving.

1 *Tim.* vi. 17. Charge them that are rich in this present *aiōn* that they be not highminded, nor have their hope set on the uncertainty of riches.

In this way we have no difficulty in understanding what St. Paul meant when in a passage, which to all appearance was too much for both translators and revisers, he said, Wherein aforetime ye walked according to the *aiōn* of this world. And I may conclude the chapter by pointing to the fact that to take World or Age as a rendering for *aiōn* in this connection is to make Scripture contradict itself. Jesus prayed not that His disciples should be taken out of the world, but that they should be kept from the evil. But the translators would have us think St. Paul to state :—

Gal. i. 4. Our Lord Jesus Christ, who gave Himself for our sins, that He might deliver us out of this present evil world.

When, however, we know that St. Paul said, Out of this present evil *aiōn*, we see there is no contradiction. Neither does he contradict himself when he urges in another that :—

Titus ii. 12. We should live soberly and righteously and godly in this present *aiōn*.

CHAPTER XIII.

AIŌNIOS

Words are like men, not only in their ancestry, and in being both better and worse than they seem to be, but also in that they are sometimes authoritatively chosen to occupy positions and perform tasks for which they are not competent.

THE work done so far may be looked upon as merely preliminary, and any success attending it but as the capturing of a few outposts of the citadel. For *aiōnios* is the word represented by the adjectives in the phrases Eternal Life and Everlasting Punishment; and the preparatory work will go for almost nothing unless it can be shown that here, too, as with *olam* and *aiōn*, the theory adopted is able to prevail.

Liddell and Scott's great dictionary dismisses the word after but very brief notice. It seems to hint that it may signify Lasting for an age, but gives no reference to such a use, otherwise we are told it is the same as *aidios*—perpetual, eternal.

But the most remarkable testimony to the supposed meaning, Eternal, is found in the work of the revisers of the New Testament. So far as I can discover, it is the one word in their estimation, and the only possible word, in the English language that is competent to translate *aiōnios*. So possessed are they with this idea that they have, as already noticed, everywhere displaced Everlasting as the representative of *aiōnios*, and put Eternal in its stead.

In doing this, it was suggested they had in their minds some thought as to a difference in signification between Everlasting and Eternal; but as neither they nor their work tells us what it is, it cannot be discussed here. Failing this, the word must be taken as synonymous with Perpetual and Never-ending, and other words and phrases used to speak of what is Everlasting.

This is the accepted meaning of Eternal, both in the mind of the public, and with few exceptions, to be noticed later, in that of scholars and writers. And although some of these probably use it with reference to the past as well as to the future—distinguishing in this way Eternal from Everlasting—they see the notion of never-endingness as much in the former term as they do in the latter. Consequently, leaving out of account for the time being the two or three writers alluded to above, who propose some such expression as Age-long, one hears everywhere the assertion—advanced with all confidence by men whose ability and authority seem warranted by university degrees and diplomas of learning—that the primary meaning of *aiōnios* is, unquestionably, Eternal.

There is no mistake, then, in saying that this is the great stronghold of the subject. And it has an impregnable look about it which, if it were in truth all that it appears to be, might well daunt us. Yet if the reader will look he shall be shown a weak place or two such as will effectually make him suspect the position to be by no means so invulnerable as it seems.

AIŌNIOS. 171

Let us listen to St. Paul :—

Rom. xvi. 25. The revelation of the mystery which hath been kept in silence through times eternal, but now is manifest.

Titus i. 2. Which God, who cannot lie, promised before times eternal.

Now any reader who is on the look-out for information, properly so called, will abruptly refuse to hearken to any such phrase as Times Eternal. And no wonder, for the adjective, instead of qualifying the substantive, actually contradicts it. The noun speaks of time, the adjective of eternity. And, indeed, we have only to define the terms to see that the words make nothing but nonsense. For time is limited duration, while Eternity is duration without end. So that St. Paul, when this matter is scrutinized, is represented as saying, The mystery which hath been kept in silence through never-ending periods of limited duration. St. Peter says his beloved brother Paul in his epistles wrote some things hard to be understood; but we may be quite sure he never wrote anything like Times Eternal.

We may as well recall just here that distinction between Eternal and Everlasting already noticed once or twice, and quoted in an earlier chapter as the definition of a scholar of repute. Eternal, he told us, looks backward to that which had no beginning; Everlasting looks forward to that which never ends. With this in view, let us look once more at these two citations from St. Paul's epistles.

In the first of them it will be seen that the Times Eternal have come to an end; for the revelation of the mystery which was kept in silence through times eternal is now manifested. In the second text the Times Eternal had a beginning; for it tells us the hope of Eternal life was promised *before* times eternal. So that we have introduced to our wonder and astonishment quite a new and unheard of kind of Eternity; an eternity which has a beginning and comes to an end!

These expressions of St. Paul are still a little puzzling to us when we have cleared them of the ambiguity which the accepted rendering imposes upon them. This is possibly because we have not made ourselves acquainted with the apostle's way of thinking. A Mystery, in his use of the word, is something which is made known to the initiated. And the "mystery" alluded to in connection with fixities and fixed times is the making known to the Gentiles the unsearchable riches of Christ. This, he says (Eph. iii. 9; Col. i. 26), has been hid in God from all fixities and generations. We may think of him as referring to the ancient philosophies, but we must not neglect to include that other Fixity, the rulers of which crucified the Lord of Glory.

As these fixities had their periods of duration, it is quite natural for him to say the mystery was kept in silence through fixed times. And once those times are set before us, with their great secret fixed from the sight of men, we can follow St. Paul without difficulty when he declares that grace was given us in Christ Jesus before the fixed times (2 Timothy i. 9); and that eternal life was promised before the fixed times. (Titus i. 2.)

To this it is only necessary to add that the context in each of the last-quoted passages proves that St. Paul was thinking as he wrote of the concealment which was characteristic of these fixed periods, during which God's secret was kept inviolate. The grace was given us in Christ Jesus before the fixed times, but hath now been manifested by the appearing of our Saviour Christ Jesus. And in the quotation from the Epistle to Titus, God, who promised eternal life before the fixed times, in His own seasons manifested His word.

In these places, then, where the word Eternal is unsuitable, and even absurdly fails to translate *aiōnios*, our own theory of the meaning of the term would seem to establish itself.

But there is another consideration which will, I think, convince the reader that the sense of never-ending duration, as applied to *aiōnios*, must be relinquished. *Aiōnios* is the adjective of *aiōn*, and in accordance with the rule and custom of language and with common sense, it is intended to speak of a thing as having the nature or quality of an *aiōn*. When we speak of a road as being hilly, we cannot mean anything else than that the road partakes of the character of a hill. So when we read of anything as being *aiōnios* we may be quite sure it is because it is thought of as *aiōn*-like. If *aiōnios* in the use of the New Testament writers means Eternal, then in their hands *aiōn* must mean Eternity. But, as we have seen, *aiōn* does not mean Eternity; *aiōn* means Fixity, or Certainty.

Even to the translators and the revisers *aiōn* standing alone never signifies Eternity. The only instances in which it is made to point that way is when *aiōn* has the preposition Unto before it, as when *eis ton aiōna* is rendered For ever. But this is only when *aiōn* is singular; when it is plural it means, not Eternity, but Ages. And seeing that the presence of a preposition or an alteration in number cannot change the essential meaning of a word, it may be repeated more emphatically and without reservation that *aiōn* in the New Testament *never* has the signification of unending duration. Consequently *aiōnios* cannot mean Eternal.

To the translators and revisers *aiōn* means World and Age. So that their way of making and using language is this: substantive World, adjective Everlasting; substantive Age, adjective Eternal. That is as though they were set to speak of a road as having the character of a hill, and called it long, or wet, or flat. To have been consistent they should have found or invented such adjectives as World-like or Age-like. But then, instead of Eternal Life and Everlasting Punishment, we should have read of Age-like Life and World-like Punishment! And the time is not distant when readers will think of Eternal, or Everlasting, as a rendering of *aiōnios* much as they think of the expressions I have just written down.

Some writers have of late thought to lighten the difficulty of making an adjective mean one thing, while the noun from which it is formed means another, by introducing such words as Age-long and Aœnial, or Aœnian. It does happen sometimes that a new word is made welcome and comes to stay. It is when it fills a felt need. But does Age-long or either of those other monstrosities do that?

Suppose we read St. Paul's surmise to Philemon about Onesimus as:—

Philemon 15. For perhaps he was therefore parted from thee for a season, that thou shouldest have him age-long.

Such phraseology as this, one may safely predict, will never be accepted by anybody except people who strangely seem to think that indefiniteness should be a main characteristic of what they call revelation. If we ask of what nature is the Age, and of what length, there is nothing in this compound of vagueness, Age-long, to supply an answer.

It is very different with *aiōnios* when we realize its true purport. Here, as elsewhere, this word, divinely spoken by the ancients, gives us clear information about that which it is used to qualify. St. Paul is thinking of the more sacred bonds that will now bind Onesimus to Philemon. "No longer as a servant, but above a servant, a brother beloved." The ties between brothers in Christ are more *aiōn*-like, more *olamic*, than those between master and slave: and the apostle's inference is that Philemon will now have Onesimus *inviolably*.

So far as we have gone, then, there is good reason for thinking the primary meaning of *aiōnios* is not eternal, but that it is used to speak of what it qualifies as having the nature of Fixity. In going the round of other texts we shall find abundant confirmation of this idea. But before doing this it will be well to have a full and lucid definition of *aiōnios* formally before us. What I offer as such will, I think, agree with every instance of its use in the New Testament, and at the same time identify it with the *olam* of the Hebrew Scriptures.

Aiōnios is employed by the writers of the New Testament to guard against the thought of internal defeat, or of injury or hindrance from without, to which what is spoken of might otherwise be considered liable. It is therefore synonymous with Indefectible, Inviolate, or Inevitable, as the nature of the case may require.

I may say that Indefectible is put in for the sake of clearness. The reader will see how it is really involved in the second term; what is perfect is so because it is inviolate to all causes of imperfection. But there are cases in which Indefectible gives the sense more clearly. It is, however, important to remember that a full account of *aiōnios* may be summed up under those two great branches of Fixity, Inviolability and Inevitableness, which we found to be characteristic of *olam* in the Old Testament.

The worth of the definition I have given can only be ascertained by looking at every occurrence of *aiōnios* in the light of it. If the texts become more intelligible, if the reader finds they do not deal with what is metaphysical and transcendental, but that they speak of things within the range of knowledge and demonstration; and if he sees that *aiōnios* does in the hands of the Hebrews who wrote the New Testament just what their own native *olam* did in the Old, he will probably think the definition just and the argument complete.

The order of procedure, in what will be considered the most important part of our work, will be to reserve the texts on Eternal Life and those generally associated with Everlasting Punishment for subsequent chapters. The others will occupy the remainder of this. There are seventeen of them, and with one exception they may be rather roughly grouped as speaking of Qualities, Things, and Processes.

The exception is :—

Romans xvi. 26. According to the commandment of the Eternal God.

In this text Eternal tells us nothing of God, except that He is of unending duration. But so, in popular belief, is all this world of men; and Eternal tells us in reality no more of Him than the word Immortal does of ourselves. To me it is impossible to conceive that St. Paul was not repeating a mode of expression with which we made acquaintance in the Old Testament, and notably in Isaiah.

Taking this to be so, and that here we have a repetition in Greek of the *olam* God, how much the word tells us. To speak of Him as Indefectible and Inviolate sets us thinking of all conceivable imperfections and mutations that would make Him less than *aiōnios*. And as we think of them all—imperfections of mind or purpose, of affection and of power, or of changes wrought by ages or circumstances, or by our own demeanour or default—as we bring them one by one before us, and this great word *aiōnios* bids us dismiss them from our creed, it cannot but be that our God and Father grows in our regard. While if it be true that we are always in danger of making God in our own image, here is an effectual safeguard. Here too is the remedy for that ignorance of God, and doubt of Him and fear of Him, which are the most prolific causes of distress in this distressful world. When we shall give up speaking of Him as Eternal, and begin to think of Him as *olam* and *aiōnios*, we shall feel it quite natural to say, or sing, O give thanks unto Jehovah, for He is good, is suitable, is just what we need, because His lovingkindness is absolute, His mercy is inviolable.

The texts spoken of as coming under the head of Qualities are the following:—

1 *Tim.* vi. 16. To whom be honour and power eternal.

2 *Cor.* iv. 17. Our light affliction, which is for the moment, worketh for us more and more exceedingly an eternal weight of glory.

1 *Peter* v. 10. The God of all grace, who called you unto His eternal glory in Christ.

Heb. ix. 14. Who through the eternal Spirit offered Himself without blemish unto God.

I do not think the first passage in this list should read as though it were merely a pious wish that honour and power everlasting should be given to God. It is rather an ascription of what is; *in* Him are honour and power eternal.

The honour is, speaking definitely, the worth or value inherent in God. And the power is governing, or dominating, power. If the context be carefully read, it will be seen that these are the very divine qualities Timothy in his work needed to keep in view; and *aiōnios* is used to express and emphasize the superlative character of them. The worth of God is indefectible and inviolate; the power is invulnerable and invincible. His value is perfect, and cannot be lessened; His might cannot be weakened, and must prevail.

It has already been grumbled about the word Eternal that one of its aggravating deficiencies is its leaving us outside of a thing, revealing nothing of inward quality. If, for instance, we could speak of an eternal man, the man, so far as any information to be got from the adjective goes, might be almost any kind of man—Alexander or Atkins, St. Paul or Demas. *Aiōnios*, on the contrary, would tell us the man was indefectible, invulnerable, and invincible. So it is when we look at the passages about Glory. Everlasting Glory puts before us something that will always endure, but it says nothing about its nature, and it gives no hint as to why it is eternal. But if we allow *aiōnios* to help us, as it was intended to do, we learn that the glory is perfect and supreme, that it cannot fade or be eclipsed or outshone, and that because of this it must always endure.

Thus a term like Eternal is in place in this connection, but only in the secondary and consequent sense to which allusion has previously been made. If we ask why

> The boast of heraldry, the pomp of power
> And all that beauty, all that wealth e'er gave,
> Await alike the inevitable hour?

the true answer is, Not so much because they are, all of them, evanescent in their own nature, as because they are not *aiōnion*, not inviolate to antagonistic forces prevailing against them from without. The glory to which we are called in Christ is eternal because it cannot fail in itself, and because no external power can effect it. But Eternal by itself could not tell us that, and it is not, therefore, an adequate rendering.

It is worse when we read that Christ, through the eternal Spirit, offered Himself without spot to God. This is a text about which there has been much controversy and much writing. The common view is that the words refer to the Second Person in the Trinity; and this idea seems to be favoured by our version, which inserts the definite article and the capital letter in the word Spirit. In the original it is simply, Who through *pneumatos aiōniou* offered Himself. For this reason, as well as because of its want of clearness, the usual interpretation is not accepted here.

A truer account of the phrase and its meaning may, I think, be obtained by thinking of a saying of our Lord addressed to His disciples: Ye know not what manner of spirit ye are of. What manner of spirit, let us ask, was that through which Jesus offered Himself to God? The answer is, A spirit impervious to all unworthy motive; and despite contumely, pain, and death, undaunted and unfailing. It was an *olam* spirit, inviolate and invincible.

The quotations in our second group, coming under the head of Things, are rather more numerous:—

2 *Cor.* iv. 18. The things which are seen are temporal; but the things which are not seen are eternal.

2 *Cor.* v. 1. A house not made with hands, eternal in the heavens.

Luke xvi. 9. Make yourselves friends out of the mammon of unrighteousness; that, when it shall fail, they may receive you into the eternal tabernacles.

Heb. ix. 15. The promise of the eternal inheritance.

2 *Peter* i. 11. The eternal kingdom of our Lord and Saviour Jesus Christ.

Heb. xiii. 20. The blood of the eternal Covenant.

Rev. xiv. 6. An eternal gospel.

I remember a doctor of divinity of my acquaintance saying in the course of conversation, The primary meaning of *aiōnios* must be Eternal, or St. Paul could not have drawn the contrast he did between things temporal and things eternal. But suppose we ask, Why are the seen things temporary and the unseen things everlasting? The answer seems to be that while the one class of things are vulnerable, affected by change and decay, the others are inviolate.

The value of seeing what is really the primary meaning of *aiōnios*, rather than fixing the thought upon a secondary and consequent meaning, will be felt in the case of every other example found in this group. Take the house not made with hands. The way to arrive at the bearing of *aiōnios* upon it is to ask what defect, or what injury, the earthly house of our tabernacle, with which the "eternal" house is contrasted, is subject to. The house of clay may crack and crumble, or it may be thrown down by violence. Before that comes to pass we find it sometimes tottering, sometimes pervious. With many of us it is a life-long struggle to keep out the weather and frustrate the forces of decay. And at last we fail. Thinking of all the burden of the flesh, we cannot but appreciate the greatness of the word *aiōnios*, by the use of which St. Paul tells us the house not made with hands is absolutely inviolate.

This, too, is characteristic of the "eternal tabernacles," which are put in contrast with the steward's own house, and the tenant's habitations into which he hopes to be received when he is turned out of his office, but which in their turn will also fail him.

An inheritance, to go on with our list, is not ordinarily a thing one would care to speak of as *olam*. A man may be heir presumptive, and even heir apparent, and yet never inherit; or if he should succeed, the inheritance may somehow be marred, or it may fall in value, or pass out of his hands. But the heritage of which the author of the Epistle to the Hebrews writes is *aiōnios;* it will inevitably be the possession of the heirs, and it will be inviolately their own, incorruptible, undefiled, and fading not away.

History shows how many are the defects and disasters to which kingdoms are liable. The government of them is often unenlightened and weak; sometimes it is altogether bad. None of them has been or is universal. They decline and fall. They are subject to insurrection and disruption, to invasion, absorption, and extinction. The use of *aiönios* is intended to guard against the thought that anything of the kind can befall the kingdom of Jesus. It is a kingdom of all *olams*. It is perfect, and will be supreme; it is a fixity as to its coming, and it will be a fixity in its reign.

The further we proceed with our examination the more apparently convincing grows the evidence as to the justness of the definition now advocated. What could be more out of place than such a word as Eternal when applied to the New Covenant? The writer of the epistle, in describing the Covenant, never thinks of laying stress upon the fact that it will last longer than the old covenant. His point is the efficiency of the New as compared with the inefficiency of that which, having waxed aged, was ready to vanish away.

A Covenant is an arrangement for making people what we call good. This the old arrangement failed to do. But Jesus is the Mediator of a better arrangement, one of which all the details and methods and adjuncts are better; so much better as to be absolutely effective for the purpose of making men good, whether that goodness be viewed as the knowledge of God, the awakening of love, or the rectification of error in thought or conduct. To say of such an arrangement that it is eternal is to say literally nothing to the purpose. The Covenant is *aiōnios*, it is perfectly adapted to the end in view, all-efficient, infallible.

And, to my mind, to put Eternal or Everlasting in front of Gospel is to disguise it. It sets us thinking of unending existence when, here almost more than anywhere, we need to be thinking of character. It is the glorious gospel of the Blessed God, such good news that, fully understood, it may well be called, in accordance with the etymology of the English words, The spell or story of God by which we are held spell-bound. The Good Tidings are the best possible; and the adjective used by St. John is intended to guard us from the thought that there can be any flaw or any danger of disappointment, or that anything can make the gospel other than it is.

The texts speaking of Processes are four in number:—

2 *Thess.* ii. 16. God our Father which loved us and gave us eternal comfort.

Hebrews v. 9. He became unto all them that obey Him the Author of eternal salvation.

Hebrews vi. 2. Eternal judgment.

Hebrews ix. 12. Having obtained eternal redemption.

It may not be exactly correct to speak of some of these, Comfort and Judgment especially, as processes. The words may point to the result of the comforting and the effect of the judging. But even so Eternal is an unworthy representative of *aiōnios*, because it does not tell us what we chiefly need to know, and what the writers intended to tell us.

Comfort that lasts for ever is beyond all question a great

gift, only our experience shows that it is not commonly enjoyed. For our help and peace it needs again and again to be renewed, through our own fault no doubt, but so it is. And the use of the adjective is to assure us that comfort, which is not only help as against sorrow, but help in every time of need, is a divine fixity; it is unfailing when we seek, and it is certain in its result.

Speaking of Judgment, Edmund Burke is reported to have said, It is the day of *no* judgment that I am afraid of! But judgment being a matter admitting of the use of *aiōnios*, he need have had no fear. Judgment is inevitable, it is a fixture. And when here it will be inviolate to all those influences of ignorance, harshness and softness, and fear and favour, which make the judgment of men imperfect always, and sometimes unjust.

But redemption and salvation are unquestionably processes; and to speak of eternal or everlasting processes is to speak unthinkingly and even absurdly. Everlasting redemption is redemption that is never completed, may we not say? and never-ending salvation a salvation whose work is never done; and so redemption and salvation that never quite redeems and never completely saves!

If this is said to be trifling, I can only let the matter pass by retorting that it is the upholders of that wicked usurper Eternal who are the real triflers. So far from being everlasting, the process of redemption is finished. The words are, "*Having-obtained* eternal redemption." And the same writer again and again pictures the Redeemer, not as redeeming still, but as seated in majesty at God's right hand; resting, so to speak, while what He has done works out its inevitable results. The redemption is a fixity; it is inviolately finished, the testimony to be borne in its own times.

And *aiōnios* applied to salvation tells us what *olam* told us in the same connection. It is the grandest *olam* of all, excepting only its Author. It is salvation that is inviolate to all search for deficiency, and invincible against all opposers. This is beautifully pictured for us at its first appearing upon earth, when one of the last true representatives of ancient Israel holds the infant Jesus in his arms. It is but a Babe of a week old that the aged face looks down upon. Thirty years must elapse before the redeeming work can actively begin, and Simeon will have gone. Hundreds, even thousands, of years must come and go before the Gentiles will have seen the light, or Israel have acknowledged the glory. But to Simeon the salvation is an absolute certainty; no accident can befall the infant life, nothing can hinder the completion of His work, and holding the Child in his arms, Simeon sings :—

>   *Luke* ii. 29–32. Now lettest Thou Thy servant depart, O Lord,
>   According to Thy Word, in peace:
>   For mine eyes have seen Thy salvation,
>   Which Thou hast prepared before the face of all peoples;
>   A light for revelation to the Gentiles
>   And the glory of Thy people Israel.

CHAPTER XIV.

"*ETERNAL LIFE.*"

> Still he found, whatsoever so-called doctrine he parted with, that the one glowing truth which had lain at the heart of it, buried, mired, obscured, not only remained with him, but shone out fresh, restored to itself by the loss of the clay lump of worldly figures and phrases in which the human intellect had enclosed it.
>
> Dr. George MacDonald.

IN this chapter and in the succeeding one the writer has again and again found it needful to pause and divest himself of preconception; and he may be forgiven for asking his readers, should the necessity in their case arise, to be on their guard against the influence of the same baneful power. I say baneful because a preconception is much the same thing as a prejudgment, or pre-judice; and that is the taking up of an opinion, or the forming of a judgment previous to the examination of evidence, and therefore really without evidence. Than this nothing can be more hurtful to the mind, nor can anything be more detrimental to clear and satisfying perception of religious truth. Yet it is much more common than is generally supposed. An acute thinker has said:—

"All men are apt to have a high conceit of their own understanding, and to be tenacious of the opinions they profess; and yet almost all men are guided by the understandings of others, not by their own, and may be said more truly to adopt than to beget their opinions."

And the reader is asked not to allow any opinion he may have adopted, or any even that he may have begotten, to stand in the way of his accepting what after due scrutiny may appear to be the meaning of Scripture words.

He will not always find it an easy task. For as nothing is more common in religious matters than preconception, so nothing is more powerful; and especially is this the case, or perhaps I should say has been the case, with the supposed meaning of *aiōnios*. Its sway has been hardly less wide than, and quite as dominating as the notion of the sun going round the world. Appearances are in favour of this latter theory, but appearances are not in favour of the former; for to a thoughtful person the idea of everlastingness is not within the scope of revelation properly so called. Yet the consequences of rejecting the meaning of endless duration, so long and so almost universally held to appertain to *aiōnios*, are such that the vision of them in the case of many of us, unless we are very careful, results in the preconceived opinion tightening its grip.

Bishop Westcott told us, in a quotation given some pages back, that eternal life is what St. Paul speaks of as Life indeed. We shall have abundant opportunity of seeing the justness of this conclusion. In the meantime let it be noted that, notwithstanding the strength and prevalence of preconceived opinions on this subject, there are only two texts that have even an appearance of speaking as though eternal life belonged to a future, and not to this present world. One of them is:—

Luke xviii. 29, 30. There is no man that hath left house, or wife, or brethren, or parents, or children for the kingdom of God's sake, who shall not receive manifold more in this time, and in the *aiōn* to come eternal life.

The coming *aiōn* refers, as we have seen, to the advent of a new order of things, not to a future world. And "this time" is the season in which the sacrifice is made. The act of self-denial brings with it immediate joy (with "persecutions") more than sufficient to compensate for what is relinquished. And the life thenceforth entered on is such as to require the use of *aiōnios* to describe it.

The second text referred to is:—

Matt. xxv. 46. These shall go away into everlasting punishment; but the righteous into life eternal.

It should be borne in mind that we have here a quotation from a parable. Now in a parable what we may call the surface meaning is not the true significance which the parable itself partly unfolds and partly veils. The commentators, or most of them, see here a picture of what is called the general judgment at the end of the world. Yet they would not say the everlasting fate of all the nations depends upon their feeding the hungry and clothing the naked. Nevertheless, this is what the scene points to if we read it as narrative and not as parable.

I venture to think the truth indicated by the parable is one that we may all easily demonstrate for ourselves; but we must leave it for the present, until we have made acquaintance with the meaning of the terms Eternal Life and Eternal Punishment.

It is sometimes said the Life may be thought of as beginning here, but that *aiōnios* is used to tell us of its continuance through endless ages. This is the old mistake, against which we have so often fought, of putting duration in the place of character. *Aiōnios* does not tell us how long the Life will continue; it tells us what kind of existence the Life is. No doubt we are all at one in hoping the Life Eternal will be enjoyed in worlds yet to come; but the contention is the New Testament writers, in their use of the phrase under discussion, never had such a meaning in view. To carry our thoughts beyond the grave they had other words, such as Resurrection, Immortality, and Incorruption.

The texts that speak of Eternal Life as a present possession are numerous and explicit. I will give a selection, and begin with the greatest:—

John xvii. 3. This is life eternal, that they should know Thee the only true God, and Him whom Thou didst send, Jesus Christ.

The Life is identical, or, at least, synonymous, with the knowledge of God and of Jesus Christ. To have the one is to have the other. If, then, it be possible to know God and Jesus in this world it must also be possible to have eternal life here. On the other hand, to read the saying as telling us that to have the knowledge spoken of is to have never-ending life brings before us something which we might perhaps take upon trust, but would not be able to prove.

St. John, in one of his epistles, speaks as though men may have eternal life without being aware of it, and that his object in writing to them is that they may know they possess it:—

1 *John* v. 13. These things have I written unto you that ye may know that ye have eternal life.

And he reports other words of Jesus that are quite as conclusive as those already quoted:—

John v. 24. He that heareth My word, and believeth Him that sent Me, hath eternal life.

The hearer and believer has something more than the blessed hope of everlasting life; he has the eternal life itself in present possession. If he does not know it, his want of knowledge of the fact arises from the habit of thinking of eternal life as being other than it really is.

So the first stage of our inquiry leads us irresistibly to look upon Eternal Life—whatever may be the meaning of the words—as something pertaining to this present sphere, and therefore something whose reality and quality we must be able to test for ourselves. And we might think, in passing, of the immense advantage this gives to those who preach about it, and to those who listen. He that believeth *hath* eternal life. This, then, is not a statement to be accepted at the word of the preacher, of the Church, or even on that of Jesus Himself; it is a declaration as open to demonstration as are the words, He who is weary is glad to rest.

But, then, it follows that eternal life cannot possibly be life in any of its ordinary meanings. In our use of the English language we habitually use the word Life in the senses of Existence, Livelihood, Life-time, and Vivacity. And the reader will see that *aiōnios* cannot fittingly and truly be united to any of these. The life-time ends, the livelihood is uncertain, the vivacity gives place to despondency. Life, in a word, is not *olamic* — it is exposed to pain, worry, and *ennui*, to decay, decrepitude, and death. So that, if our conclusion as to the true meaning of *aiōnios* be correct, the word Life in the phrase we are trying to understand cannot mean life.

And, indeed, the use of the New Testament compels us to look upon Life in this connection as being altogether a poetical and figurative expression. The Young Ruler who came to Jesus asking—

Mark x. 17. Good Master what shall I do that I may inherit eternal life?

and the "sheep" of whom Jesus said—

John x. 28. I give unto them eternal life,

were in the vigorous possession of literal life when the words were spoken. Yet Jesus said He came that they might have life. And these sayings of His require us to think that in the words Eternal Life life does not mean life, any more than eternal means eternal. This is the same result as that which followed from the impossibility we felt of applying the great word *aiōnios* to life in its ordinary meaning.

It may almost seem to some readers that an apology is due for asking them to read anything so obvious as the last two paragraphs. But do we all see where exactly we are? If the ground upon which we have taken our stand be *aiōn*-like, then eternal life means neither immortality nor heavenly bliss. But it points to a state or condition in this present world absolutely impervious or inviolate to the slings and arrows of outrageous fortune, and to all the influences which so often make life a perplexity and a trouble of heart. Are we prepared to believe that such a condition exists, that it is accessible to us all, and that it is capable of "scientific proof"?

If we are not, if we are surprised such a question should be asked and incline to answer it in the negative, then it seems probable, on the face of it, that we have something to learn about the true nature of the Good Tidings, one of whose most constant themes is Eternal Life in Jesus Christ our Lord.

In pursuing our inquiry, we will take it for granted that Life in the phrase before us is a figure of speech—a figure, we must not forget, made use of not by Greeks, but by Hebrews writing in Greek. This thought brings before us the Hebrew Scriptures, and the probable fact that the New Testament writers were reproducing in their own work something familiar to them in that of Moses and the Prophets. And in the earliest pages of the Bible we find this:—

Gen. ii. 17. In the day thou eatest thereof thou shalt surely die.

Eve and Adam, disregarding this injunction, did eat, and they did not die in the day they ate of it. There have been many attempts to explain the apparent contradiction. All, however, that is needful for clear comprehension is to think of death in this denouncement as a condition beset with evils from which the forfeited condition was free. In plain and unpictorial language, they exchanged a higher state for a lower.

In after-times Moses, speaking to the children of Israel, exclaims:—

Deut. xxx. 15. See, I have set before thee this day life and good, and death and evil.

Reading his words with precision, we see that he so speaks as to define the terms: the life, even the good; the death, even the evil. "Life" to Moses, from whom most of the greatest Biblical ideas descend, meant evidently a condition that is good, and "death" a state that is evil.

This figurative use of life and death is quite common in Hebrew literature, and many, and of much interest, are the examples that might be given. Two more will, however, be sufficient for our immediate purpose. One is:—

Ezek. xviii. 20. The soul that sinneth it shall die.

The other is one of numerous indications that *aiōn*-like life is, in substance, an Old Testament idea :—

Psalm cxxxiii. 3. There Jehovah commanded the blessing, even life *ad-olam*.

Passing on to the New Testament, we find, as might be expected, considering who wrote it, the same way of speaking continued. Thus St. Paul says :—

1 *Tim.* v. 6. She that giveth herself to pleasure is dead while she liveth.

But the most notable instance in the New Testament, and by far the most instructive, occurs in the parable of the lost son :—

Luke xv. 32. This thy brother was dead and is alive again.

The contrast drawn is plainly not between existence and non-existence, but between a lower state and a higher. A young English prodigal departing for the "far country" will sometimes speak of his anticipated experience there as "seeing life." Jesus views it as a life so unprotected, unsupplied, and insufficient, as to be worthy only of the name of death. Experience proves Him to be right;

and experience also proves Him to be resurrection; that He came that men may have life, and that they may have it abundantly.

It is a remarkable fact, and one among many others testifying to the uniqueness of the Bible, that no other literature uses the words life and death in this sense. We at times speak of a place as dead-alive, and of some physically-wrecked creature as being in a condition of living death; but not even we English, despite our well-known superiority in matters religious, have as yet attained to the custom of talking about wrong-doing and harmfulness as Death, and of obedience and beneficence as Life.

And it is most worthy of notice that the writers of the New Testament found no hint of such a habit of thought in the Greek language employed by them to make known their message. Jesus and St. John and the rest put into Greek what they found in their own sacred literature, just as they did in the case of *olam*. And the fact is another instance of the inadequacy of the advice given by a prominent Churchman to the effect that nothing is needed for the elucidation of the New Testament except a knowledge of Greek and the use of a Greek lexicon.

But, leaving this, we may assure ourselves that we have seen the meaning as well as the origin of the use of Life and Death as New Testament parables or figures of speech. Life is a condition that is good; it is what, in fact, in English may be spoken of as Well-being. The perception of this significance throws light upon an otherwise almost incomprehensible saying of Jesus :—

Luke xii. 15. A man's well-being consisteth not in the abundance of the things which he possesseth.

And this interpretation will prevent us from preaching or speaking about the wages of sin, which is death, as being death physical, death spiritual, and death eternal; we shall see it to be, what it demonstrably is, an evil condition of life.

It is well to remind ourselves that the words Eternal Death do not occur in the Bible. When we think of what they would imply we cannot but be glad they do not. Death, in the literal sense, would tell of death out of which there would be no resurrection if *aiōnios* were used to qualify it. In the figurative sense it would mean an evil condition of existence inveterate and inviolate; and this, as we shall see in the sequel, would be a conception wholly out of harmony with New Testament thought.

Another thing important enough to be noticed in this connection is that the phrase Spiritual Life has no Biblical authority. It is very commonly used in religious talk and writing, but, in the absence of any exact definition of the terms, it is, like For ever and ever, too vague to be of real service. If the reader will put the three expressions, Eternal Life, Spiritual Life, and Inviolable Wellbeing, before him, and listen to them, he will not have any difficulty in deciding which of them is the most informing and, therefore, the most worthy.

Taking Life, then, in this figurative use of the word, as equivalent to Well-being, we may go on to ascertain whether the men of the New Testament were justified in speaking of it as Life *aiōnios* or Life *olam*. In other words, Is the condition they thus speak of available in this present world, and is the quality of it demonstrably indefectible and inviolate?

To answer the question we must first know what the New Testament has to say about the Well-being, what it is in itself. We can find no formal definition of it, such, for instance, as those by means of which theologians set forth their dogmas. These are as absent from the pages of St. John and St. Paul as they are from those of Tennyson and Browning. But description of another kind is both rich and abundant. And, what is often lacking in those other methods, the path to possession is so plain, that the way-faring men, which means the men who *fare* in that path, though fools, need not err therein.

In seeking the information just now needed, we cannot do better than recall the great text :—

John xvii. 3. This is life eternal, that they should know Thee the only true God, and Him whom Thou didst send, Jesus Christ.

These immortal words tell us that inviolate Well-being consists in the knowledge of God and of Jesus Christ. Bishop Westcott, in his commentary, says the verb does not denote completed knowledge, but a striving after growing knowledge. Whether this might not meet the case of the Agnostic we need not stay to inquire. But supposing he should still cling to the notion that God is unknowable and striving after knowledge of Him quite useless, he will readily acknowledge that to know Jesus as He is depicted in the New Testament is quite within our reach. And even if he should hold the opinion that the Gospel stories are not historical, this will make no difference, for Eternal Life is made to depend upon the knowledge which, in whatever form, is there set forth.

But, according to Jesus, the knowledge of God is involved in the knowledge of the Christ whom God hath sent. For He says:—

John xiv. 9. He that hath seen Me hath seen the Father.

We are all agreed that we may know Jesus as delineated, and almost the first thing we learn in making acquaintance with Jesus is that, in His opinion, to know Him is to know God.

What, then, is Jesus as portrayed for us in the gospels and epistles? Is it possible to give a description or definition of Him as to which all sorts and conditions of Christians—Trinitarian, Unitarian, Catholic, Protestant, Conformist, and Nonconformist—will be perfectly at one? It is possible. St. Peter, speaking in the house of Cornelius, talked of Him as One

Acts x. 38. Who went about doing good.

As I have intimated, there will be no dispute as to the fitness of St. Peter's words. Some readers may think them insufficient perfectly to describe the Christ of God; none will say they are incorrect. Others will think them supremely and comprehensively true, and that in the recognition of the fact they proclaim and in fellowship with it the Churches will some day forget all their differences.

But if to see Jesus is to see God, it follows that God also is One who goes about doing good. And this exactly accords with the teaching of Jesus everywhere about God. He does not refer us to imaginative or philosophic thought, nor, except in illustration and for corroboration, to the visions of the seers and the priestly symbols and external nature. He bids us look within, and learn the character of Deity from the strongest altruistic feeling known to our hearts, the "likest God within our soul."

Matt. vii. 11. If ye, being evil, know how to give good gifts unto your children, how much more shall your Heavenly Father.

This is another way of saying God is Love. If we could ask St. John how he defined those terms, I venture to think he would say, seeing he was a Hebrew, By God I mean the Supreme, and by Love I mean Desire, Purpose, and Effort to do good. He that abideth in these abideth in the Supreme and the Supreme abideth in him.

Deep down in all our hearts there is a conviction, not clearly recognized it may be, and not always acknowledged, that this is indeed the supremest of all things human. And there, too, whatever our creed may be, is the often dimmed and yet inextinguishable hope that before and over all things superhuman is an infinite Desire, an unchanging Purpose, and an all-prevailing Endeavour to work the best. This was the faith of Jesus. What He saw supreme in the universe He made supreme in His own heart and life. And in Him the trinity of Love—the desire, the purpose, the endeavour—were unaffected by rejection and hate, and rose undiminished out of death, even the death of the Cross.

Seeing all this, we cannot but feel that we are part way to the comprehension and to the possession of inviolate well-being. But only part way. For to know Jesus, even to strive after growing knowledge of Him, includes more than understanding what He was and what were His secret and method. The word Know must come into line with, and signify just as much as words in other texts, which I will now proceed to quote :—

1 *John* v. 11, 12. God gave unto us inviolate well-being, and this well-being is in His Son : He that hath the Son hath the well-being ; he that hath not the Son hath not the well-being.

John iii. 36. He that believeth on the Son hath inviolate well-being.

John vi. 53, 54. Verily, verily, I say unto you, except ye eat the flesh of the Son of Man, and drink His blood, ye have not well-being in yourselves. He that eateth My flesh and drinketh My blood hath inviolate well-being.

Looking at these three sayings, we come to see that the words, Hath the Son, Believeth on the Son, and Eateth My flesh and drinketh My blood, must be exactly equivalent to *Knowing* the Son, for they all result in the same condition of inviolate well-being. It is most important to note this, for nothing is more common than to speak of believing as one thing, and of eating the flesh and drinking the blood as altogether another thing; whereas they are but different methods of pointing out the one way to "eternal life." There is but one inviolate well-being, and there is but one method or means of obtaining it ; and what that is these texts discover to us.

The last of them is the most valuable and decisive ; and, contrary to ordinary opinion, it is not the most difficult. It is a striking instance of the fact, and this is why I allude to it before noticing the passages in order, that in reading the New Testament we should remind ourselves that the surface-meaning is simply illustrative of the real significance. This, in a measure, is true of the other texts; and unless we keep it in view we may not read so wittingly as we otherwise should.

In asking what St. John means by his expression Having the Son, we may be sure he uses the word in the sense of possession. But then we have to remind ourselves that there is more than one way of possessing a thing. Some people possess books, and value them solely because they are first editions, or because they present something remarkable in the way of binding or printing. They give them a conspicuous place in glazed cases, it may be, secured with lock and key, and know nothing and care nothing about their contents. Still they say they possess them.

Other people there are who can recall a Book, worthy of the capital letter, which came to them, perhaps, in exchange for a few pence, from a second-hand bookstall, whose contents so took hold of them and mastered them as ever after to influence their thought and their conduct. We hardly know whether to say they possessed the book or the book possessed them. But it is clear that in a true sense the book was not of their lives a thing apart, as is the case with the book-owners spoken of in the last paragraph. Here there has been fusion, and there is permanent union; and there can be no doubt as to which kind of possessing St. John refers when he says, He that hath the Son hath the Life.

So there is a kind of surface-meaning belonging to the word Believe against which we need to be on our guard; for no more fatal error can be committed than the allowing men to think that they can share in a thing simply by believing. Common sense and experience constantly prove the contrary. We believe in *Bradshaw's Guide* and in the train, but that does not take us to the journey's end. We have the most unshaken faith in the efficacy of food, but we are not saved from hunger and faintness unless we eat. So believing in Jesus is not, and does not of itself result in, oneness, in fusion, with Him. It is the action consequent upon our faith, our adherence, our faithfulness to the teaching and to the example of Jesus, that brings us into possession of the life inviolable.

And this holds good about the saying which speaks of eating the flesh and drinking the blood. The surface-meaning cannot be taken, for it is past dispute that no one ever did, or ever will, eat the flesh and drink the blood. Jesus Himself, in the discourse from which the words are taken, points to His teaching as being to men the source of life. But there may, perhaps, be difficulty in understanding how He could fitly speak of our eating His words. If so, a well-known saying of Lord Bacon will help us :—

"Some books are to be tasted, others to be swallowed; some few are to be chewed and digested." Jesus' words must be "chewed and digested." In the language of a familiar collect, we are to read, mark, learn, and inwardly digest them. That is to say, of course, we are to assimilate them, make them a part of ourselves. Eating and knowing, adhering, beholding, and possessing, are different ways of speaking of one and the same thing, and that is fusion with Jesus. In plain language, needful for Western folk if they would understand what the Easterns veil in parable and similitude, we are to hearken to and obey, and be like Jesus, who believed God to be working for the best, and who Himself went about doing good.

We may view the "hard saying" in another way. The Flesh of Jesus we may think of as the vehicle of manifestation in our earthly life of what He is, the means of making known what is in His heart, and what He sees to be the heart of God. The Blood, we may say, is the vigour, or energy, of Love which He poured out unto death. The Flesh and Blood we are to "eat" and "drink," that is to say, the manifestation of supreme desire and purpose to do good, the energy of Love expended to the utmost, is to be our sustenance. When perplexed and pained by mystery and evil we are to live upon that. And when we feel, as all men do at times, a yearning so to live as to lay hold on the life which is life indeed, we are to find the satisfying of our hunger there.

There are good Christian men who think these words of Jesus point to a miracle wrought in the Eucharist by which the bread and wine are changed into the Body and Blood of our Lord; others, equally good, thinking that impossible and incredible, say He is to be eaten only after a "spiritual" fashion. Some there are—and who, knowing them, will say they are any the less Christian?—that will not eat the bread nor drink the wine; and much is still made of these differences of opinion, and in the days, the dark days gone by, crimes were committed by the Churches because of them. Do such variations in thought matter so very much after all? At any rate, our chief concern should be that the only convincing evidence of our having eaten the Bread of

Heaven, after whatever manner, is that in so doing we have attained to that higher state where uncharitable and bitter feelings do not invade; where, in lowliness of mind, each Christian man (and may we not say each Christian Church?) counts others better than self, and where all things are ordered after the pattern of Him who went about doing good.

Each of these illustrative words of union brings us, then, to the same conclusion. Eternal Life, or, as we put it, Inviolate Well-being, is a life of trust and active beneficence based upon and resulting from our belief in and our adherence to the supremacy of love, upon our having grown incorporate into the Son of Love. It is not possible to think that such words as Know, Have, Eat, and Adhere can mean less than union in desire, purpose, and endeavour. And that this is the true idea the New Testament seems to show wherever we open it. What the spirit of Christ was we have seen, and it is written, If any man have not the spirit of Christ he is none of His. What this world of woe and want needed Jesus came to give; and what the eager expectation of the groaning and travailing creation waiteth for now is the unveiling of the sons of Love.

It is sometimes remarked that if the idea of life as probation issuing in everlasting happiness or unending misery were a Biblical idea, we should naturally expect that every New Testament speaker or writer would take his part in clearly and emphatically announcing it. As much may be said of this present topic of indefectible well-being. But in this case we do not come upon one or two instances of apparent proof which upon examination turn out to be no proof at all. On the contrary, we hear Jesus and His apostles unanimously and explicitly proclaiming Eternal Life to be what we have tried to depict it. This direct testimony must now come before us. After looking at it we shall only have to inquire if the Life Eternal, viewed as Inviolate Well-being, can be properly said to be *aiōnios;* or, in other words, whether the well-being is demonstrably inviolate.

Let us first of all look again at the case of the man who came to Jesus asking what he must do to inherit eternal life. It was said to him, If thou wilt enter into life keep the commandments. From time immemorial those commandments have been compressed into two, Love to God and Love to man. So that to love God and Man is really to live. The questioner was also told that if in this matter of life he would be perfect, he was to sell all that he had and give to the poor. In these words, and in the further counsel to "Follow Me," Jesus seems to hint at what He had done Himself: He was rich, but emptied Himself for the sake of the "poor."

Either this same man or another asking a similar question wanted to know the meaning of loving one's neighbour. He got for his edification the parable of the Good Samaritan. Reading that parable, and remembering the question that originally led to its being spoken, we see that the man who shows mercy is laying hold on the life eternal; and that the priest and the Levite, notwithstanding their ecclesiastical position and their creed, are not "ordained to eternal life," and are judging themselves unworthy of it.

In that other parable of Sheep and Goats some go into life eternal. The "Sheep" have been kind to the poor;

they have fed the hungry, and have clothed the naked. They are surprised to find that in doing this they have ministered to the necessities of the King, and that they share in His glory. And no doubt many who live to do good are not fully aware of the heights to which they rise; they do not know that they have eternal life. But one thing they do know, or come to know as the years pass on, they have found a source of happiness more full and unfailing than anything else they have known, a memory which always smiles, and a strength for the future which is as though the Well Done had come across the gulf to meet them. Every good action, wrought from worthy motives and at cost to self, is a breath of life eternal, of indefectible Well-being. This is demonstrable; so also is what our version calls Everlasting Punishment.

I must pass by a multitude of allusions teaching the same lesson, although in them the words Eternal life do not occur. Just one quotation, as a specimen of others, may be given :—

James i. 27. Pure religion and undefiled before God, even the Father, is this, To care for the fatherless and the widow in their affliction, and to keep himself unspotted from the world.

Unspotted from the world's way in such matters, seems to be the apostle's meaning, judging from the context. And note the significance of the reference to God as the Father.

St. Paul, writing to Timothy, speaks of contentment, and exhorts him to flee from the love of money, and to follow after the qualities needed for the service of man, that so he may "lay hold on eternal life." He then proceeds as follows :—

1 *Timothy* vi. 17-19. Charge them that are rich in this present *aiōn*, that they be not high-minded, nor have their hopes set on the uncertainty of riches, but on God who giveth us all things richly to enjoy ; that they do good, that they be rich in good works, that they be ready to distribute, willing to communicate, laying up in store for themselves a good foundation against the time to come, that they may lay hold on the life which is life indeed.

St. John is equally clear, and even more emphatic :—

1 *John* iii. 14-17. We know that we have passed out of death into life because we love the brethren. He that loveth not abideth in death. Whoso hateth his brother is a murderer ; and ye know that no murderer hath eternal life abiding in him. Hereby know we love, because He laid down His life for us : and we ought to lay down our lives for the brethren. But whoso hath this world's goods, and beholdeth his brother in need, and shutteth up his compassion from him, how doth the love of God abide in him?

No doubt there is here something of hyperbole. A man may hate his brother, and yet not murder him. And not every man is required to lay down his life for the brethren. But the bearing of the quotation upon the nature of the life which is well-being is very apparent. Here is a desire and purpose to do good so strong as not to allow self to stand in the way. It is not a matter of word, but of deed. We know the measure of the love of Jesus, because He laid down His life for us. To shut up our compassion from one in need is akin to hating him ; and the culmination of hate is murder. Inviolate Well-being is not found in such a condition. He who loveth not his brother abideth in "death"; but he who does love hath passed out of "death" into "life."

The reader may probably by this time think he has had enough, and more than enough, of quotation in support of the theory that by eternal life is really meant Well-being, and well-being that, unlike ordinary being or life, is not exposed to invasion and disaster. And nothing more has to be done now except to ask if this really is so. Is the well-being *aiōnios*? Is it an *olam*, a Fixity, in the sense of being impervious and inviolate?

In trying to answer the question we must think over the causes that make ordinary life a weariness, or a burden, or "not worth living," and consider whether or no the Well-being set before us in the New Testament is impervious to them, fixed beyond their power to injure. Only one or two of them will be mentioned here; but readers can easily make the same inquiry for themselves with respect to any others that may occur to them.

To the man who is possessed by the conviction that Deity is supreme Desire and Purpose to do good, stronger, more enduring than all, the *olam* Love, it does seem manifest that much of the weight and weariness and unintelligibleness of the world will have disappeared. He will still be pained and troubled, and often perplexed. But it will be by processes; he can have neither doubt nor fear as to the result. He will not always understand how everything can be of Love, and through Love, and unto Love; yet he is assured that Love will be all in all. Pessimist a man cannot be whose soul is held by this conviction. He who believes hath entered into rest. The earth will be full of the knowledge of the glory. Meanwhile we can ask :—

> "Oh Life! without thy chequered scene
> Of right and wrong, of weal and woe,
> Success and failure, could a ground
> For magnanimity be found
> For faith 'mid ruined hopes, serene?
> Or whence could virtue flow?"

Equally sure is it that the Life Eternal knows nothing of that strangest of ills, the boredom and discontent of life spoken of as *ennui*. No true follower of Jesus of Nazareth can be in danger of so much as a yawn in premonition of that complaint. And it is remarkable, when we come to think of it, that anyone should continue to suffer in such a way with so simple and pleasant a remedy always within reach.

> " Lady Clara Vere de Vere,
> If time hang heavy on your hands,
> Are there no beggars at your gate?
> Are there no poor about your lands?"

Everybody knows Tennyson; but I will quote some other lines that may not be familiar, even to a Methodist reader. I dare say there may be those who will think them to savour of enthusiasm, if not of rant; but the lesson is there all the same. They are from one of the favourite songs of a strange figure flitting through these islands during the greater part of the last century, trying to do good in every way open to him. He preached in almost every town, if not every village, of England, Scotland, and Ireland. In drawing-rooms, to "pretty triflers" and "butterflies of fashion," his text was, Ye serpents, ye generation of vipers, how shall ye escape the damnation of hell? Among the "heathens" of Moorfields and Kingswood it was, Come unto Me, all ye that labour and are heavy laden. He wrote commentaries; grammars in four or five languages, and tracts on almost every conceivable religious, moral, and political topic; he established schools, and set up free dispensaries. Last, but by no means least, he made a fortune, by the sale of books and so on, of nearly a hundred thousand pounds, and he gave it all away. This was his song, or part of it :—

> "In a rapture of joy, my life I employ
> The God of my life to proclaim ;
> 'T is worth living for this, to administer bliss
> And Salvation in Jesus' name."

It is not given to us to reach such altitudes as this, nor is it necessary to our eternal life that we should. If the reader remembers, it is not the completed knowledge but the striving after growing knowledge that brings inviolate Well-being. And surely enough of that is possible for all of us to raise an impregnable defence against the demon *Ennui*.

To speak for a moment of another, even of the "last enemy." Is the eternal life, now we understand something of its true nature, invulnerable to death ? The men who first taught, and others who have done what they could to follow the teaching, declare it to be impervious to the fear of death, and to the doubt of immortality. They tell us the best preparation for the end is the remembrance of having tried to go about doing good. They say they find no relaxation of the *olam* arms as the enemy draws near. And they cannot believe that Love, the supreme desire and purpose to work the Best, can ever be the God of the dead.

But the only method of demonstration open to those of us who do but look on is to try for ourselves.

P

CHAPTER XV.

"*EVERLASTING PUNISHMENT.*"

All warnings and threatenings are of the fire of love which consumes evil. Seen in the light of divine faith and love, every providential dispensation, every chastisement or affliction, is part of the mighty famine which draws starving humanity home to the bosom of the Father.—*The Gospel of Divine Humanity.*

AS no doubt will be generally expected, the first text to come before us under the above heading will be:—

Matt. xxv. 46. These shall go away into everlasting punishment, but the righteous into life eternal.

A comparison of successive versions of the English Bible shows the first part of this quotation to have undergone what we may call a softening process. In the earliest it was Everlasting Torments. Then Torment became Pain. In the A.V. Pain was altered to Punishment. This the revisers allowed to stand, only they changed Everlasting into Eternal. All this looks like objection to the ancient opinion, and uncertainty as to the precise meaning of the original.

We might perhaps content ourselves with seeing in the words an assertion that Punishment is *olam;* it is a fixity, a certainty. And this is a truth which in these days especially needs proclamation. For in the fading of old theories, the thought may arise of there being nothing to fear at all. But there will be wrath and indignation, tribulation and anguish, upon every soul of man that worketh evil. This is demonstrable; the soul that sinneth dies.

Taking it for granted, however, that it will be desired to treat the text before us exhaustively, we shall want to see what exactly is meant by punishment being a fixity. In other words, we want to know the definite significance of *aiōnios* as applied to the term which in the text under consideration is translated by the word Punishment. And we cannot do this unless we make acquaintance with the substantive *aiōnios* is used to qualify.

When we track the word through the various places of its occurrence, which the reader shall be asked to do directly, we find that it tells rather of Check or Hindrance than of Punishment, and that probably the best English word for it is Restraint. This meaning fits all the instances in which it is found; it gives a much clearer sense; and it reproduces in the New Testament a turn of thought familiar in the Old. Three more cogent reasons for accepting it could not be found.

I have said it gives a clearer meaning. The well-known words of St. John, for example, puzzle us until we make the suggested alteration:—

1 *John* iv. 18. There is no fear in love: but perfect love casteth out fear, because fear hath punishment: and he that feareth is not made perfect in love.

Fear hath punishment! What is the meaning of that? Fear may be said to "punish," using the word in rather a slangy way, him who is oppressed by it; but it is because fear *restrains* from the perfect confidence resulting from perfect love. It is better therefore to read, Fear hath restraint. Fear holds a man back from rest and peace.

We may make the same change, with similar profit, in the other instances, and there are only two of them. One is from St. Peter :—

> 2 *Peter* ii. 9. The Lord knoweth how . . . to keep the unrighteous under punishment unto the day of judgment.

According to preconception punishment comes *after* judgment, and that consideration should induce those who are still swayed by it to join with other people in altering punishment into restraint, at least in this quotation. The change brings the words into harmony with the illustration by means of which the Apostle introduces his subject: If God cast angels into dungeons to be reserved unto judgment . . . He knoweth how to keep the unrighteous under restraint unto the day of judgment.

In the other case alluded to—

> *Acts* iv. 21. And they when they had further threatened them let them go, finding nothing how they might punish them, because of the people; for all men glorified God for that which was done—

punishment seems to be quite a wrong word to use. The object of the rulers was to hinder Peter and John from continuing to teach the strange doctrine with which they were filling Jerusalem. They would, perhaps, have restrained them by imprisoning, or even by killing them, had they dared. As it was they could do nothing but threaten, and finding no other way of restraint, they let them go.

As already intimated, this thought of restraint seems to have been brought over from the Old Testament. At all events it may be illustrated by references there. The following passage from one of the prophets, for instance, will, if carefully pondered, help us in more ways than one :—

Ezekiel vii. 19. Their silver and their gold shall not be able to deliver them in the day of the wrath of Jehovah ; they shall not satisfy their souls, neither fill their bowels, because it hath been the stumbling-block of their iniquity.

I beg leave to suggest that Stumbling-block should be relegated to a museum of translators' curiosities, and that Restraint should be put in its place. A stumbling-block hinders by throwing one down, but the word so rendered implies keeping one back, as an impervious hedge or an unscalable wall would do. And Iniquity stands for the word used by Cain in his great and bitter cry, My punishment is greater than I can bear. The prophet Ezekiel really says punishment, or the consequences of sin, may be hindered, or kept back for a time, by silver and gold. We can all see how true it is still that by the possession of wealth men are able to restrain and keep back some of the troubles resulting from wrong-doing. But in the day of the wrath of Jehovah it will no longer avail them.

Returning now to the text in St. Matthew's Gospel, with the information we have gained, we feel obliged to turn Punishment into Restraint. And if we ask the question, Restraint from what? the answer seems to be obvious. The fault of the goats, or, to speak more exactly, the *little kids*, is selfish disregard for the needs of others ; unlikeness to Him who went about doing good. From this it would appear they are to be restrained. Or if not from selfishness in itself and primarily, then from the pleasure and satisfaction fancied to belong to selfishness. But take away all the pleasure and profit of wrong-doing, and how long will it continue?

In another parable we have a picture of the circumstances in which one of these "kids" finds himself in the other world. Here on earth he clothed in purple and fine linen, but he did not make to himself friends out of the mammon of unrighteousness; and there he has none to receive him to the inviolate tabernacles. From the other side of the gulf nor from his own does there come so much of comfort or of peace as might be illustrated by a drop of water on the tip of a finger! The restraint is complete; and it does not seem altogether improbable that the desire expressed about his brethren marks the beginning of a better state of feeling. Perhaps for the first time in his history he is concerned about the true well-being of his fellow-men.

We have seen that Eternal Life is a condition of well-being capable of being proved. So it is with what is put in our Bibles as Everlasting Punishment. Jesus is not speaking of something transcendental, beyond experience, to be taken solely upon trust; He, as in the manner of the Hebrew seers, is calling attention to something patent and verifiable, and only too apt to be forgotten or ignored. This is undeniably true of the beginnings of the inevitable restraint awaiting the pleasures of selfishness; and granting the continuance of life in future worlds, all the rest may be logically argued. The man concentred all in self is, beyond all dispute, a *wretch*. If he be not as yet altogether wretched, it is because the "stumbling-blocks of iniquity" are not yet gone. But how must it be to find oneself where there is no wealth, no wine, no pleasure of "flesh," no flattery, and no veil to disguise the naked spirit, where a great gulf is fixed between a man and comfort from without, and where for self the whole surrounding is a fire of pain? Then, we may think, selfishness must be inevitably restrained; and this I cannot but take to be the meaning of what has been hidden by the words Everlasting Punishment.

It has seemed to many writers an unanswerable argument that *aiōnios* being used to qualify both Punishment and Life, and this in the same sentence, they must necessarily be of equal duration. Wesley's note on the text is according to this idea:—

"Either, therefore, the punishment is strictly eternal or the reward is not; the very same expression being applied to the former as to the latter."

To me the wording of this note leaves the meaning of *aiōnios* an open question. But when we remember that *aiōnios* is not significant of duration at all, the argument so often built on the use of the word in this text falls to the ground. There is a fixity of restraint, and there is a fixity of well-being; as to whether either or both be endless, *aiōnios* in itself gives us no hint, that not being its business.

This is the general meaning. But, entering into particulars, the unprejudiced reader will probably see that *aiōnios* is capable of, and indeed requires, differing shades of meaning when applied to these two Fixities. It guards against the thought of interference. But the idea of interference with well-being starts another line of thought from that suggested by interference with restraint. In the one case we are set thinking of what may alter the character of the well-being, so that it will not be well-being. *Aiōnios* guards against that, and declares the well-being to be inviolate. But interference with restraint implies something occurring to prevent its infliction, or to hinder it from accomplishing its work. *Aiōnios* guards against such an implication, and declares the restraint to be inevitable and irresistible.

Our next field of observation is a statement by St. Paul:—

2 *Thess.* i. 7-9. The revelation of the Lord Jesus from heaven with the angels of His power in flaming fire, rendering vengeance to them that know not God, and to them that obey not the gospel of our Lord Jesus: who shall suffer punishment, even eternal destruction from the face of the Lord and from the glory of His might.

The words mainly requiring our attention are "Eternal destruction." But, in passing, I may say the tyrannical preconception has been at work in other parts of the quotation. I must ask the reader to take it from me, or to apply to some scholar for confirmation, that what we read as Rendering Vengeance is really the Judge of all the earth *doing right*. And "suffer punishment" is *paying* to justice or right. But we need not linger over these expressions.

Eternal Destruction is just one of those phrases no seer or revealer of religion could possibly make use of. It is nothing less than a contradiction in terms. Eternal destruction is a destruction that never ceases from destroying, and therefore never really destroys at all. We may be sure St. Paul never wrote anything like that. What he did write was something comprehensible and quite credible.

"EVERLASTING PUNISHMENT." 217

He uses the word translated Destruction in another saying, and from its use there we may derive the light we need to illumine the passage before us.

I refer to—

1 *Cor.* v. 5. To deliver such an one unto Satan for the destruction of the flesh, that the spirit may be saved in the day of the Lord Jesus.

Now the flesh in the individual was not really destroyed in the sense of being put an end to. We meet with him later on, not disembodied, but still in the flesh and restored to the Church. What is evidently meant is that the flesh was to be dethroned and displaced from the dominating position it had usurped over the spirit.

This illustration will probably be accepted as decisive. The persons spoken of by St. Paul in the former passage were oppressors of Christians. They were men who knew not God and who were disobedient to the Glad Tidings. It is more than credible that injury of innocence and ignorance of love must be displaced by the perfect revelation by the King in His glory, or as St. Paul has it, The Lord Jesus in a flame of fire. From such evil positions men cannot but be driven into confusion and shame by the vision of the Face and the glory of the enduring strength. This is *olam;* it is inevitable.

It is of great interest here to recall the fact that St. Paul himself had passed through an experience of this kind. He, too, was once a persecutor and disobedient to the gospel. And he had been "destroyed"; he was displaced, as we may all read, by the revelation from heaven of the Lord Jesus in a flame of fire. True, he does not now picture some kindly Ananias ministering to the displaced;

he leaves them where they have been driven. But the point is, there is nothing in the word to tell of that condition as one of endless misery or everlasting damnation. Jesus speaks of restraint, inevitable from selfishness; St. Paul of inevitable displacement from ignorance and from the exercise of hatred. Both of these inevitable states are in accord with the Glad Tidings. And both agree with the Hebrew method, so often referred to, of showing the reasonableness and the demonstrableness of truths and facts, so often forgotten in this world of delusion and illusion, or treated as unreal.

It has been argued that the thought of everlasting punishment is necessary in view of the possibility of men continuing to sin for ever. That such a possibility may be seems to be suggested by a text, the only one of the kind, to which some attention has already been given:—

Mark iii. 29. He that shall blaspheme against the Holy Ghost hath never forgiveness, but is in danger of eternal damnation.

The revisers, having adopted a different reading, give us, Is guilty of an eternal sin. This clearly looks like sin that is everlasting. For, discarding the significance of endurance, and taking only the fixity sense of *aiōnios*, we have here to choose between the thought of sin, which is fixed in the sense of being inevitable, and sin which is fixed in the sense of being inviolate or inveterate. Or, rather, we have no choice; the sin cannot be thought of as inevitable, for it has already been committed when Jesus speaks. There can be no doubt, I think, that He meant to say, Hath certainly not forgiveness, but is subject to inveterate sin.

Yet a prolonged study of these words has convinced me that not even here is there any declaration of everlastingness, although, of course, it does not follow that what I may have to say will convince others. But the solution seems to lie in the word translated Forgiveness. That word properly means Deliverance. Jesus did not say, in announcing His commission, He hath sent Me to proclaim forgiveness to the captives, but, He hath sent Me to proclaim deliverance to the captives. We may, then, correct the passage whose drift we are trying to elucidate, and read, Hath not deliverance for certain, but is guilty of inveterate sin.

Now a little consideration serves to show that Deliverance is what I may call an *outward* word. It speaks of a work effected by power acting from without; and the statement of Jesus is to the effect that in such a case as this external help is out of the question. We have only to look at the nature of the sin spoken of to see that this is so. Some sins are caused by ignorance, and men may be delivered from them by an access of light. Others are the result of passion, or of the dominance of the flesh, and, as St. Paul has told us, men may be released by the "destruction" of the flesh. But this sin against the Holy Ghost was not the result of either ignorance or passion; it was a sin of choice, of the will; it said Jesus in doing good was animated by an "unclean" spirit; it deliberately declared good to be evil, and light to be darkness. Is it not fitting, then, to speak of such a sin as sin *aiōnios*? To outside effort, whether exerted in what the translators call this age or that which is to come, the Jewish or the Christian *aiōn*, the sin is plainly inveterate. But, even so, to speak of it as either everlasting or unpardonable is, I submit, to speak without warrant. The will that creates the condition has it in its power to alter it.

I said this is the only text of the kind; but there is in the Epistle to the Hebrews one that is somewhat similar. If in reading it we adopt the marginal suggestion of the Revised Version, the text will need no comment, and it will illustrate, and I think confirm, the view taken of the text from the Gospel.

Heb. vi. 6. It is impossible to renew them again unto repentance the while they crucify to themselves the Son of God afresh, and put Him to an open shame.

Before we pass on I cannot but record my judgment that the misreading of these texts is one of the many evils we owe to the persistent tendency towards exaggeration in religious things which comes of preconception on this particular subject. Many people have been made insane by these texts. Multitudes of others have been sorely troubled, because they have feared the guilt of the "unpardonable sin" was upon them. They need not have been so. The man who thinks he has so transgressed, and grieves about it, has abundant proof that whatever may once have been the case he is not now subject to inveterate sin.

The only expression remaining to be considered is Everlasting Fire. What really lies behind the English words? The phrase as it stands is, like some others we have noticed, unsatisfactory in itself and contradictory in some of its applications. An everlasting burning is one whose work is never completed. Yet the fire by which Sodom was consumed is called Eternal, although it has been extinct for ages.

This reference, and others that might be noted, suggests the idea that in the use of the word Fire we have still another instance of Old Testament thought and language reproduced in the New Testament. If we turn to the Hebrew writers we cannot but see, what our own knowledge of fire tells us, that in their thought to burn a thing is to destroy it in the sense of putting an end to it. This is so patent that it does not seem necessary to give a long list of passages in illustration of it. One great text must be quoted because of the question to which it is of all things necessary to find an answer. I speak of the declaration of Moses:—

Deut. iv. 24. Jehovah thy God is a devouring fire, a jealous God.

The question is, What does God devour? Surely not men, women, and children; for that was attributed to one of the false gods, association in whose worship was denounced as the worst of errors. The question may be answered in this way: God devours what He is jealous of. If the further query should arise, Of what is God jealous? the reply, on the lines of the language we are now considering, will manifestly be, God can only be jealous of that which supplants Him in the affection or regard of those whom He loves. Our idols, our sins, anything that tends to exclude Jehovah, who is Love, from the chiefest place—to these the God of us is a consuming fire.

So that while this great Hebrew poet saw in fire an illustration of a destroying agent, painful and irresistible in its action, as no doubt the illustration suggests, he also saw what is thus put an end to is Evil; this, I think, is apparent. Thus we should expect to find in the New Testament some such truth as is indicated by the words of Moses, and by sayings of the prophets, two of which I will also adduce :—

Isaiah iv. 4. When the Lord shall have washed away the filth of the daughters of Zion, and shall have purged the blood of Jerusalem from the midst thereof by the spirit of judgment, and by the spirit of burning.

Mal. iii. 3. But who may abide the day of His coming? . . . for He is like a refiner's fire . . . and He shall sit as a refiner and purifier of silver.

Going on, then, to the New Testament, we find first of all John the Baptist announcing the advent of the Christ, and speaking of Him and of His work in such words as these :—

Matt. iii. 10. Every tree that bringeth not forth good fruit is hewn down and cast into the fire.

Matt. iii. 12. He will burn up the chaff with unquenchable fire.

Matt. iii. 11. He shall baptize you with the Holy Ghost and with fire.

Now it is in reading these texts, and the similar words of Jesus about the burning of the tares, that we specially need to be alert and careful. If not, we shall come under the power of the preconception that the Baptist and the Christ are in these passages speaking of the burning up of human creatures, and that will prevent us from obtaining the help the texts are able to give us toward the elucidation of those other passages in which men are undoubtedly spoken of as being cast into or sent into fire.

Let us ask ourselves why, in the name of common sense, if of nothing holier, we should for a moment be influenced by a judgment which in one breath bids us believe that sinners are burnt up like chaff and tares, and in the next that they are not burnt up at all, but kept in being in fire for ever? With unbiassed minds, we should think of chaff and tares, interfering as they do with the perfection of the wheat, and incapable of being turned into wheat, as illustrative of evil things, which can never be any other than evil, such as errors, sins, and foolish notions. There will be weeping and gnashing of teeth over the destruction of these, and the overthrow of harmful preconceptions preventing the outshining of the truth. There always is! True, the parable speaks of sons of the kingdom and sons of the evil one, and that looks as though persons were referred to. But again it is necessary to remind ourselves that it is not an Englishman who is speaking, but a Jew, and the Hebrews commonly used language of that kind about things as well as about people. A flash of lightning or a spark was to them a son of fire. Besides, if we are to understand the words, Let both grow together until the harvest, as spoken of men, what are we to make of the command which, on one side of things, says, Compel them to come in, and on the other, Come out from among them and be ye separate?

The words, Let both grow together until the harvest, sound, to my ears, like the voice of one who knows the invincibility of truth, and can view the sowing of evil teaching with equanimity, and forbid its forcible uprooting, lest in the endeavour the good should be injured; sure that in the working out of the fixed order of things, in which both grow together, the evil will ultimately perish, and the true shine forth in unclouded glory. That this is so is seen in the experience of the ages. Had men possessed the faith of Jesus, persecution because of opinions would never have been heard of, and the truth would have been nearer its crown.

Our inquiry thus appears to suggest the conclusion that the sentence on the goats points to some painful and resistless agency for the destruction, not of men, but of evil. If we reject that conclusion, the only alternative meaning of fire must, so far as I can see, be the utter destruction, burning up, and putting an end to of the goats, as fire puts an end to the chaff and the withered tares. But I am unable to find in Scripture any support for such a theory as that. Fire must, indeed, represent a destructive agency, but the present investigation appears to show that it is not man but the sinfulness of man which is to be burnt up by fire, just as in other texts we found that sinfulness was to be restrained and displaced.

There is another saying of Jesus to be read and inwardly digested before we are in possession of all His teaching on this subject :—

Mark ix. 47. And if thine eye cause thee to stumble, cast it out: it is good for thee to enter into the kingdom of God with one eye, rather than having two eyes to be cast into hell; where their worm dieth not, and the fire is not quenched. For every one shall be salted with fire.

In these words Jesus advises His disciples to cast away from them all sinful tendency and occasion of transgression. It is better for them to do so, He says, than to be cast into Gehenna—into the unquenchable fire. Then He goes on to say, For every one shall be salted with fire. Every one, I take it, must mean every one. But not all are cast into Gehenna. Therefore when He says, Every one shall be salted with fire, He includes those who escape Gehenna by casting from them the sinful tendency; and He must mean that either by the pain of self-sacrifice, or by the action of the unquenchable fire, every one shall be salted with fire. In other words, the object in view is in both cases, in that of the unquenchable fire as in that of self-denial, the vanquishing and the destruction of sinfulness.

So far, then, this passage is in harmony with the view suggested by the others. And further confirmation comes when we ponder the illustration used by Jesus, and seek an answer to the simple question, What is salt used for? Preconception at once hastens to reply, Things are salted to preserve them from corruption. But let us pause, and remember we are not now dealing with the habits and customs of a bacon-eating people. There is not a particle of evidence anywhere in the Bible that salt was ever used to pickle things. What we find there is such a saying as, Can that which is unsavoury be eaten without salt? and the command, Every sacrifice shall be salted with salt. Preconception will say again, In hot countries meat soon gets bad, and salt was added to preserve it. But as soon as the victim was killed it was burnt on the altar, and salt could not be needed for any such purpose. Besides, some of the offerings were of meal, and salt was to be mixed with these.

If we put preconception on one side we realize the custom must have been instituted to teach and enforce the lesson, too easily forgotten, that men must offer to God what is, so to speak, savoury and palatable to Him; they must not offer what is not acceptable to themselves.

The universal use of salt is to season. And does it not seem natural for us to think that when Jesus said, Every one shall be salted with fire, He meant to imply that we all shall be "seasoned," or made acceptable to God, and not that some of us will be, if I may use such an expression, pickled in fire for ever.

Could we altogether divest ourselves of prejudice and preconception, and remember that in such a text as this we have a specimen of an Oriental style of teaching, we should understand Jesus to be simply trying in pictorial and emphatic fashion to show that it is better to suffer by resisting temptation and overcoming self than by the stings of conscience and the loss of peace, and the other painful results of falling into sin. Better the strict way of duty than the Valley of Achor for a door of hope. But, either by the one way or the other, Every one shall be salted with fire.

Does the use of the word Unquenchable make it necessary for us to think of the Fire as being everlasting as well as inevitable? So it is often thought and said. But let us scan the word, not that we may alter its meaning, but that we may discern its true bearing. If we call to mind how some are said to quench the violence of fire, and that we may quench the fiery darts of the wicked one, we shall, I think, perceive that Quench is what I have called an outward term. The thought in it is that of putting out a fire by external force; unquenchable, therefore, speaks of a fire that cannot be thus extinguished.

To describe a fire that burns "for ever and ever" we should require an adjective other than unquenchable—some such internal word as, for instance, Undying. The meaning of Everlasting, which has been given to *aiōnios*, makes the fire both inextinguishable from without and ceaseless from within. But that is not the true meaning of *aiōnios*, and what the Bible really says of the burning is that no force opposed to it can prevent its kindling or put it out. He shall burn up the chaff with inevitable and irresistible fire.

Thus as in the previous chapter we found no expression equivalent to Everlasting Life, so in this we can discover nothing which speaks definitely of Everlasting Punishment, and nothing whatever that could justify the use of such phrases as Eternal Death, Everlasting Torment, or Endless Misery. On the one hand, the Greek adjective used in all the texts does not mean Everlasting; on the other, Greek adjectives which do beyond question possess that meaning are never once used in this connection. What we do find is, what we have so often said we might expect to find from Seers whose business it is to teach religion, matter of observation and insight, of experience and demonstration. It is so much more like a Seer to tell of the forgotten, or the ignored, which is yet open to proof, than it is to speak of the unknowable, and to require that what he says shall be taken on his authority. So he declares wrong-doing to be Death : that is an evil condition of being. And selfishness does not achieve that greater joy for which it hoped and toiled; it results in irresistible restraint from joy. The coming of the Son of Man in His glory, or the revelation of the Lord Jesus in a flame of fire, means inevitable restraint for the selfish, and inevitable displacement for the ignorant and the disobedient. Sin is followed by pain, so certain, so irresistible, and so keen, that it is spoken of as inevitable and unquenchable Fire; while, if we allow the figures of speech to have what appears to be their full meaning, sin will be "burnt up" by the fire itself has kindled. And if we conceive of sin as Error, no one can doubt that this will be so.

All this the Seer finds in the experience of life on earth. It is part of the unchanging purpose running through the ages. And what he sees here of the uncompleted work of these processes, and of the fact that evil-doers are able to maintain some of the "stumbling-blocks of iniquity" up to the very end, impels him to believe in a life beyond this, where the Restraining, and the Displacing, and the Burning will still go on. But he does not say they will continue for ever and ever. A Seer cannot speak of processes that never end.

CHAPTER XVI.

CONCLUSION.

Alleluia; for the Lord God Omnipotent reigneth.

SO far as the scrutiny of words and phrases goes, our task may be said to be completed. For looking back over what has been recorded, though I am conscious of many defects, and of my incapacity for perfection, I cannot find that anything has been omitted. But on such a subject, and at the present time, it is perhaps desirable to speak of the conclusions about what we call the Last Things to which our inquiry seems to lead; and especially as some of these, and notably the greatest of them, have partly indicated themselves as we have gone along. Whether what I have to offer will be acceptable or even interesting to the reader, I cannot tell; but it occurs to me that any man past middle age, who has spent many years in the study of one particular subject, may be thought to have something to say that is worthy of a hearing. And this is all I ask.

Alexander Pope tells us how on a certain occasion he put what he had to say into verse, rather than prose, and that for the following reasons. Principles and so on, thus written, will, he thinks, strike the reader more strongly at first, and be more easily retained by him afterwards; and though, as he says, it may seem odd, it was nevertheless true that he found he could express himself more shortly in this way than in prose itself. I have ventured to think these notions applicable to myself, in my degree. Hence the lines that will follow. I need only say about them that each stanza is intended to set forth some separate thought bearing upon this great question; that they have been many times revised, not with any intention to "polish" them, but in the endeavour to make the thought adequate and clear, and that criticism on any other ground except this is deprecated.

Matt. xxv. 46. These shall go away into everlasting punishment.
John xii. 32. And I, if I be lifted up from the earth, will draw all men unto myself.

Did John and Matthew disagree
About His teaching, as do we?
Or, writing statements of such note,
Were they unconscious what they wrote?
And did they think this great twinlight,
Lit by their Master for the night,
Would but mislead our hopes and fears
Through all these eighteen hundred years?

Among God's angels, Paradox
Is called to minister; and mocks
At our infallibility
Lest we be gods too easily!—
Lest in the journey of our life,
Through Nature's splendour, and her strife,
We see no greater god, nor turn
Our humbled souls to seek and learn.

Both John and Matthew knew the ways
Of seeming-contradiction's maze.
For Jesus blended chieftaincy
With service and humility;

And He Earth's estimate reversed,
Said first was last, and last was first,
And showed the glory of the Cross,
And loss in gain, and gain in loss.

Had we, like John and Matthew, heard,
Would word have seemed opposed to word?
" What maketh Heaven that maketh Hell "
Both John and Matthew knew full well ;
But saw a meaning more complete
Than Love's success and Love's defeat ;
And in the words of future fate
They found no cause for fierce debate.

What God hath joined let no man sunder.
Could we commit a greater blunder
Than decompose a glory sent,
Use part without its complement,
And look at truth in coloured light?
Say, what would be our earthly plight
Did we with our diurnal sun
As men with holier light have done?

The sun is evermore a god :
He rises, spreads his rays abroad,
And we refer to his correction
The doubt that foiled the lamp's inspection.
Is Christ, then, less divine than he,
That we should judge His theory
By our poor light, and trust, and teach,
Our comment more than His plain speech?

Whence has man's preconceived opinion
Such wide and absolute dominion?
We say that mind is God's reflection,
But is God ever in subjection?
Folds He His wings in indolence?
Shrinks He from change, or such expense
As comes from brooding o'er the waste
In hope the void may yet be graced?

"FOR EVER AND EVER."

More kings are crowned by wish than wit;
And gods are throned, and demons flit
Before Imagination's eyes,
At Hope's behest, or Fear's surmise:
And man against his own projection
Is loth to suffer insurrection,
Though other gods, and demons, claim
Regard and test in Truth's great name.

True thought of God, or Christ, or kings,
Conclusive demonstration brings;
Obtains a perfect fealty,
An undivided monarchy.
But Peace, awaiting truth, demurs
When wishes are interpreters;
And fears, misgivings, contradictions,
Disturb, and evidence, our fictions.

"John's unto Me means happiness."
Suppose we hear and acquiesce;
While Matthew's terror, we agree,
Shows endless, hopeless Misery.
How firmly throned must be our notion
To find no tremor of commotion
Whene'er we to our minds recall
That John, who heard Christ speak, wrote All!

We sing a Heaven of cloudless skies,
Unbroken rest, and tearless eyes.
But Heaven is not all happiness
If Hell be ever merciless.
Or else what change must come in dying!—
Forgetfulness, or petrifying,
Till all dear memories are flown,
And saintly hearts are hearts of stone!

That word of Matthew's—chastisement—
Through eighteen hundred years' descent,
Reveals to all who care to scan
How man would punish guilty man:

Dark ages, when inhuman ire
Doomed to the torture and the fire ;
Weak ages, too, whose evildoer
Had less infliction than the poor.

Eternal chastisement, and life ;
Did John and Matthew know our strife
About that word's significance ?
Did gesture, or revealing glance,
Fill them with thoughts of endlessness
Or of the spirit's wider stress ?—
Of truth unveiled when this life ends,
Or truth that all our thought transcends ?

Is there a grave for Memory,
Or dimness in Eternity ?
Can there be less than endless sighings
O'er Christ-betrayals, Christ-denyings ?
Can God obliterate a sin—
Replace it by what might have been ?
Can He from evil men, self-wrecked,
Avert His own designed effect ?

All men, All things ! Must we misread
Lest Christ's own word to licence lead ?—
See only the believing Few,
The Called, the Gentile with the Jew ?
All men, John heard, or so he saith,
And Christ for All men tasted death ;
And All have sinned ; and All may come ;
Why only here must All mean Some ?

The sword was drawn by Simon's hand ;
The fishers drew their net to land.
" But man is more than sword and fish,"
And is not drawn against his wish."
And more than fisherman is He
Who said, I will draw all to Me !
Can we suppose that Jesus meant,
Drawing until His force was spent ?

"FOR EVER AND EVER."

Were Christ incarnate happiness,
No need to prophesy success.
But He, the Man of Sorrows, Scars,
Who with our inclination wars,
Who brings no beauty for alluring,
No word, of wealth, or ease, assuring;
How can He gather to His side,
Us who have seen and crucified?

Yet Peter, James and John, attendant,
Beheld their Lord arrayed, resplendent
'Mid darkest gloom, the cross in sight,
Whose dread would all our smiles affright !
O Joy ! O Christ, whose inward glory
Shines forth in all Thine earthly story !
O World, thou yet shalt dance with mirth,
For there is wealth to end thy dearth !

When Christ would fight, man's soul to win,
What mighty forces strengthen Sin !
How Flesh, with all its keen desires,
Will traitor play when Sin conspires !
And Ignorance by Christ defaming,
While Sin its promise is proclaiming,
Doth summon Hate, as Sin's ally,
To scorn and scourge and crucify !

But in the contest which ensues,
If Sin its strong allies should lose?
If in the dread eternal burning
There should for Flesh be no discerning
Of such small store as tips a finger,
For any thirst that still may linger?
If Sin to Flesh no joy can bring,
Where will it look for triumphing?—

To Ignorance? Essential light
Is not as day which ends the night,
Yet cannot pierce the caverned haunt
Where darkness still its reign may vaunt.

And Christ is Light, and darkness quails
When light's adaptive power assails ;—
The sun which drives it to its lair,
The searching lamp which follows there !

If hate of what is good arises
From Ignorance and its disguises ;—
Its power to veil Love's self with gear
Of penury, and pain, and fear ;
Then when the soul at last shall waken
To find its thought of things mistaken,
When every mirk and mist shall fly,
Then, it would seem, that Hate must die.

" Evil, be thou my good." If man
Should thus resolve, accept the ban,
The mercy scorn, the light bedim,
How could the Christ draw all to Him ?
And how could we the praise accord
He claims as universal Lord ?
If Sin, or Death, divide the throne,
Christ King of kings we cannot own.

Is man forever free to choose,
And every bond of law refuse ?
Or does he toil, and fight, and rest
Just as the motive may suggest ?
With every influence away,
Wills he much more than moulded clay ?
Then where the strongest lure shall be,
There will abide the victory.

All unto Christ, to righteousness,
To joy like His ; not sorrowless,
Not as all chastisement had ended !
When once our wills with His have blended,
Can Sin and Cross, so interlinked,
Become by distance indistinct ?
The nearer Him the clearer they ;
The clearer then the more dismay.

"His chosen ones forsook and fled"!
Oft as the story there is read
Do John and Matthew feel no stings?
And men befouled with viler things,
Tempters', and tyrants, devilries,
When they shall see as Jesus sees,
Can they escape an endless shame,
The deathless worm, the quenchless flame?

What homage then shall Sin obtain
When all its heritage is pain?
When all its pain forever moans
For that which none but Jesus owns?
And Jesus still will be His name,
To-day as yesterday the same!
And *Christus Consummator* will
Be *Christus Consolator* still!

But it has been objected to me that a man may be abundantly satisfied with some production of his own, and may even think it absolutely conclusive, while other and clearer eyes than his may see it to be clumsy and ineffective, or, perhaps, vaguely speculative and tentative. Be it so. Yet in this matter which so nearly concerns us all there are some things which are quite clear and quite sure; and taking it for granted they have not just now been seen, I shall no doubt be forgiven if I seek the aid of prose to point them out.

All preachers—ministerial and lay—in the Church to which I have the honour to belong are under obligation to believe the doctrine of everlasting punishment. Now, to many at the present day this is felt to be a cross—if not a stumbling-block—of a very real kind, and I think needlessly so. It was Robertson of Brighton, if I recollect aright, who said, The difficulty is how not to believe it;

and I can sympathize with that declaration. Yet, after all, the real difficulty is neither in believing it nor in not believing it, but in *defining* it. This I am persuaded no man on this earth is capable of doing; and for very obvious reasons. And when we come to think of it, what a blessed thing it is that we are not bound to believe any man's definition of this doctrine, and that we are not obliged to make any definition of it for ourselves! For in the one case we should have to accept the results of incapacity, and in the other we should be obliged to attempt the impossible! I have never yet been able to discover why it should be thought necessary to confine truth to any particular set of words and sentences. If the career of Churches and the history of doctrine teach anything unmistakably it is that truth cannot be hemmed in, and at the same time cannot be injured. We come with our definitions very much as the young man in the Prophet's vision came with his measuring line to set out the bounds of Jerusalem. And what was said then is specially applicable to truth—Jerusalem shall be inhabited as towns without walls. Jehovah will be unto her a wall of fire round about.

So with this doctrine of everlasting punishment. We may, as I think, see that it is true; only we must take care not to contend about the words, for they are not Biblical words. We may use words that are Scriptural, and say, The worm dieth not; or, There is a great gulf fixed; or we may use other words, and say some of the painful consequences of sin cannot but continue, and there cannot but be an everlasting distinction between man and man—between the Son who never left his Father and that other son who did and was driven back by stress of famine. This may be found in the Bible, and it may be logically argued; but to go beyond this is to totter where we have neither Scripture nor reason to help us.

And this leads us on to another thing, which seems equally clear and equally certain. The doctrine of everlasting punishment, as formerly and almost universally defined, is in our time altogether discredited and powerless. It may still lurk about some of the older haunts of belief or opinion; but if it does it is very much like ghosts, as to which people are partly incredulous and partly afraid.

So absent from pulpit and school has been this old form of the doctrine during the last twenty years that many people who have grown to maturity during that period do not really know what it was like. Here is an extract from a sermon by Jonathan Edwards on Sinners in the hands of an angry God:—

"The God that holds you over the pit of hell, much as one holds a spider or some loathsome insect over the fire, abhors you. . . . God will have no other use to put you to, but only to suffer misery. . . . God will be so far from pitying you when you cry to Him, that it is said (?) He will only laugh and mock."

Now Edwards was in many respects a great man, and he had a heart. When he said all this he was standing behind an open Bible, and he thought it was all there; and the tears were not far from his eyes. Yet the Bible was innocent. Such language, such sentiments, such illustrations, cannot be found there. What, then—and this is a question that very much concerns those of us whose business it is to teach truth—must have been the deadly power of that preconception, or prejudice, which could induce the man of intellect to believe such horrors to be taught of God, and impel the man of heart to ascend the pulpit and declaim them to his congregation until one of his own officials sprang up and implored him to have mercy upon the people? And the strangest thing of all was that the preacher—so far as one can understand—was bound by another preconception to believe that some of the people were predestined to be reprobates, and could not help being "damned"!

This last remark may lead some readers to say Edwards was a Calvinist, and that this would account for many things. But let us read an extract from a sermon by an Arminian :—

"Is it not common to say to a child, Put your finger into that candle; can you bear it even for a minute? How, then, will you bear hell fire?"

That it was common to say this to one child, not by its father or mother, the present writer can testify, and he could tell of nights of terror that followed. And this is from Wesley, whom a little while back we heard singing in a rapture of joy! There can be, notwithstanding, no doubt as to the goodness of his heart. According to one of his biographers there can be no doubt either of his knowledge of the letter of the New Testament. When he was at a loss to remember the English he could always quote the Greek. And this makes the matter the more remarkable, for there is nothing there that could warrant him in using such language — there is nothing there to teach him that children are in danger of hell fire at all! Children are of the other sphere; and we are told that unless disciples, apostles, and evangelists are like them they cannot enter the kingdom of heaven. Wesley has been called the most apostolic man who has lived since the days of St. Paul, and I, for one, have no doubt he was; yet he could talk calmly about it being a common thing to ask children to put their finger into the fire that they might feel what hell was like. What need, then, there is for *us* to be sure we know what, perhaps, we only think we know, and to unlearn whatsoever is not of truth! This is the value of the example set by the Hebrew Seers; they spoke only of what can be demonstrated or logically argued.

But I know of some readers who will be quick to say, just here: Jonathan Edwards and John Wesley were unauthorized teachers, schismatics, you know; what else could you expect? Well, my friends, you have authority. Opening the Book of Common Prayer, and turning to the Burial Service, you read, This service is not to be read over any that die unbaptized. Here is plain proof of succession from Augustine, for that notable Father is reported to have proclaimed that all babies who die unbaptized go into everlasting torment. But, then, in this matter Augustine did not derive from St. Paul. St. Paul, as we know, could be choleric on occasion, and he would have done for such a statement as this what he wished certain troublers of the Galatian churches would do to themselves. Also in the Burial Service we may read, Deliver us not into the bitter pains of eternal death. And in the Athanasian Creed, which is to be said or sung on Christmas Day and other festivals, we have this, among other things, Which faith except every one do keep whole and undefiled without doubt he shall perish everlastingly. The only remark one feels called upon to make about this quotation is that "without doubt" it is a statement incapable of proof.

Now all this about Edwards and Wesley and the Book of Common Prayer is not brought in here out of any love for raking up things that were better drowned in Lethe and forgotten; nor for any such unprofitable business as the flogging of dead horses. Our business is really momentous.

It will be remembered that something has been said in the course of our investigation about the common exaggeration of the sterner side of things in religious matters. Every reader knows there are two sides in the Bible; one of them I will speak of as the influence of Love, and of the other as the influence of Fear. But what every reader of the Bible does not know is that the Bible regards the former as immeasurably the more worthy of honour and infinitely the more effective. It would very much surprise some people if they heard this assertion, because they have derived many of their ideas about the Bible from religious publications written on the assumption that Scripture makes most of the influence of Fear. We have a curious but indubitable proof that the Bible rightly puts first things first, in the change that has taken place in our treatment of lunatics and criminals. Something also has been done in this connection for the sinners whom Jesus loved, especially in the work of the missions in our large towns. But there is a grudge against the saints of another order in that they have not done, and are not now doing, for the sinners all that the Bible suggests.

R

In almost all books of theology with which I am acquainted there is still a tendency, I am very willing to add an unconscious tendency, to exaggerate the sterner side and to minimize the other. The Fear of the Lord becomes the Terror of the Lord. And this serves to illustrate the mischievousness of the tendency; for fear is a reasonable thing, but terror is unreasonable, and it is not used in the Bible in this relation. Again, in such a text as, Fear him which after he hath killed hath authority to cast into hell, the pronouns are printed with capital letters, and it is otherwise read as though Jesus were, without any doubt, speaking of God and not of the devil. And the Greek word rendered sometimes by Destroyed, sometimes by Lost, and sometimes by Perished, is often asserted to have no less a meaning than hopeless and irremediable ruin. Yet it is that word which occurs in the great saying of Jesus, The Son of man came to seek and to save that which was Lost; and in what is said about the prodigal, He was Lost and is found.

At the same time words which, if allowed to stand as they are, and to speak with their natural meaning, appear to point to the salvation from sin of the whole human race, are limited in their scope and lessened in significance. Professor Beet, in his latest book, has laid us under obligation by stating that the Bible contains no clear assertion of the endless misery of the lost. This, coming as it does from a man in his position, adds greatly to the debt we already owed him. But Dr. Beet himself does not appear to be quite free from the tendency just now under review. One can say this with the less hesitation in that he sets so good an example by carrying out the Methodist rule of telling other people what he thinks wrong in them. Speaking of the prediction of Jesus about drawing all unto Himself, Dr. Beet says Christ might correctly speak thus even though He foresaw that in many cases His influence would be ineffectual. Now Dr. Beet or any other scholar would tell us that this word, translated Draw, in every other place of its occurrence in the New Testament means *effective* drawing, drawing all the way; and I think the reader will see that this appears to be an instance in which a word is not allowed to have its full and proper meaning, because it conflicts with a theory about the other side of things. Bishop Westcott's comment on the prediction is this: The phrase must not be limited in any way. We must receive it as it stands.

Or take an example on the other side. Dr. Beet adopts, he does not beget, the "argument" founded on the words, Good were it for that man if he had not been born. The idea is that the words are a proof that Judas could never attain to a better state of things. For if he did, what would be his at last would be so great that under any conceivable circumstances, even with ages of suffering before him, it must have been better for him to be born, and possess it, than not to be born and lose it. The fallacy, and it is a glaring one, is in the implication that an unborn being can be capable and conscious of loss. Our own homely proverb says, What the eye does not see the heart does not grieve. And where there is neither eye nor heart nor any consciousness, nor even existence, there certainly cannot be any sense of loss.

I have no wish to pursue this subject farther than is absolutely necessary, though the field is wide and tempting. As we have seen, the best of men are apt to make mistakes, and from the best of motives. And until we can disabuse our minds of the notion that Fear is the diviner power, and that men can be driven by Fear where they can only be drawn by Love, we shall go on making them. It is because of this foolish notion that the texts of Scripture of both kinds have been treated in the way they have. And I should like, before passing on, to assume a little boldness and daring, and therewith challenge all concerned to contradict and confute the assertion that hardly a passage in our English Bible of the sterner sort appears there in a form which is not exaggerated; and of texts of the other kind I should like to say how to my apprehension they appear to be so clear and so full, that it is not in the power of human language to make them greater than they are.

We shall all agree, I think, in saying that this idea of the supposed necessity for making most prominent the influence of Fear, found its culmination in the doctrine of Everlasting punishment as formerly, and almost universally, defined. And we shall agree further that this, the head and front of its offending, is in our day a powerless thing. Who can doubt it? Where are the preachers who talk to their people on the lines of the quotations I have given from Edwards and Wesley? What would become of us if we did so talk? There is no need to ask what would become of our congregations. It may be said that those other phrases are still in the Prayer Book. So they are. But many of us who use it, at least in part, have long ago ceased to say, Deliver us not into the bitter pains of eternal death.

And as to the Athanasian Creed, and especially the "damnatory clauses" thereof, from what I am able to gather in a rather wide acquaintance with those who are required by rubric to use it, it is looked upon very much as a connection of the family who cannot be altogether ignored, but who is kept out of sight as much as possible, and talked about as little as may be, and viewed generally as one who has done something to be ashamed of. Let the thoughtful reader ask himself why this is so, and why in the nature of things it was to be expected? And why the honoured head of the family, if I may carry on the figure, the sustainer, and protector, and comforter, is that clause of another creed, I believe in God the Father Almighty?

And I should like to ask the thoughtful Methodist reader to peruse and compare two verses which I will quote from his hymn-book :—

> "Nothing is worth a thought beneath,
> But how I may escape the death
>   That never, never dies;
> How make mine own election sure,
> And, when I fail on earth, secure
>   A mansion in the skies."

> "Stronger His love than death or hell;
> Its riches are unsearchable;
>   The first-born sons of light
> Desire in vain its depths to see,
> They cannot reach the mystery,
>   The length, and breadth, and height."

These verses are by the same writer, and they are in the same metre. They are, if I may judge, equally good as poetry, being smooth and tuneful, and all the other things critics say about what is good. And they have both of them that ring (or swing, is it?) for which the Wesley hymns are unrivalled. Yet mark the difference in the fate of them. One is more confident and jubilant than ever; the other may still, for all I know, stammer a little, but for most of us its voice is lost. And does anyone need to ask the reason? It is not "change of taste," or "the spirit of the age"; nor is it "depraved dislike." The reason is in the verses themselves. One of them is truth, and truth which we are more and more coming to verify; the other does not belong to that category.

There is no need to say more in support of the assertion that this doctrine, in its ancient form, has lost its power. It hath pleased Almighty God, of His great mercy, to take out of our hands a weapon much relied on by our fathers, but never forged in heavenly fires. And it is very natural that some of us, and most of all the elders, should shrink from realizing it and acknowledging it, lest harm should ensue. The motive is a very laudable one, but the timidity is unnecessary. The battle is the Lord's, and Jehovah Sabaoth cannot suffer defeat.

We must not ignore the fact that the influence of Fear is often salutary; but then it must be a fear that can be reasoned, and not an indefinable and incredible Terror. In insisting upon the latter, the former has been neglected. Yet the preacher who will bring to bear upon his people the influence of a fear which will appeal to their reason or to their affection, and which they can see for themselves must be a fact of human experience, will do far more good than he ever could by threats of never-ending torment. And of warrant for reasonable fear we have abundance in the Bible. The wages of sin, the abiding wrath, the recompense of reward for every transgression, and the sorer punishment, to mention only a few of the phrases giving ground for the use of the influence of Fear, can all be demonstrated, if only we have a clear perception of the meaning of Bible words. So can the solemn fact, more solemn than any imaginary terror can ever be, that neither atonement nor pardon will avert some, at least, of the painful consequences of sin.

But let us have done with terror. This as a means of bringing the world to God has been tried to the very uttermost. It has had every advantage of opportunity and accessory that human power and imagination and eloquence could give it. When the Churches separated, or split into sections, and became so divided as to make communion impossible, and separate burying-places essential, the Terror maintained its hold on almost all sides of the disruption. There have been times when it has merited every fearsome epithet in the language, from savage ferocity on to diabolical cruelty. And yet it has failed, altogether failed.

Meanwhile that other power—the influence of Love—has not been fully tried. It is no wonder. Yoke Love and Terror together to accomplish some task, and they will not attempt it. Instead of doing that they will turn to and fight each other! In this case the fight has lasted long, but there can be no misgiving as to the victory. Stronger His love than death or hell! But it is only of late that we have come to see that love is something more than attribute; that it is what we have no other word for than substance, or essence, and that all other attributes are qualities of Love. Yet for a hundred years and more we have been singing, His heart is *made* of tenderness; and for fifty generations GOD IS LOVE has been in the

New Testament; and ages before that was written the Hebrews were chanting, His loving-kindness is *olam*. But it is a characteristic of our times that this truth is manifesting itself, and commending itself to our conscience in the sight of God. It is visibly breaking through every If and But that have been set up in limitation of it; yes, and through all thought of it as caused or conditioned, fettered by sin and set free again by the Cross. More people than ever before believe the two great commandments to have been really written by the Supreme finger. And is there any one of us, is there any Agnostic or Pessimist even, who will refuse to say that Love is best, and that to rule by love is the ideal rule? We may not always, alas! allow our creed to govern our conduct, and many may not know that agreement with what has just been said is an endorsement of the teaching of Moses and of Jesus, but the fact is clear and certain. The truth of the supremacy of Love, defined as desire, purpose, and endeavour to do good, is great, and it prevails; but the dogma formulated by the notion of a need for terror has not prevailed.

About these two things, the truth of everlasting punishment, and the want of truth in the doctrine as formerly defined, one has felt able to write with confidence. They have been spoken of as both clear and certain. But it is not possible to do that with regard to a third and final topic. Here, as in the verses some pages back, I only speak interrogatively, speculatively; not asserting anything, but submitting for consideration what, to my own mind, seems to have the appearance of certainty. No doubt what has to be said is involved in the interpretation given to *olam;* but that interpretation is, of course, on its trial, and may, conceivably, be found untrue.

Let us begin at a point where all Wesleyans, at least, are agreed. We never object to sing such lines as these:—

> " The word Thy sacred lips has past,
> The sure irrevocable word,
> That every soul shall bow at last,
> And yield allegiance to its Lord " ;

or these :—

> " He sits at God's right hand
> Till all His foes submit,
> And bow at His command,
> And fall beneath His feet."

We all sing them, and we will do ourselves the justice of saying that we all sing them with understanding and in accordance with John Wesley's declaration in the Preface to the hymn-book, that no word is used except in a fixed and determinate sense. We may, indeed, say that we allow ourselves, sometimes, more laxity of expression in singing poetry than we should in dealing with Biblical statements; but then we are reminded that these verses are paraphrases of Scriptural words. And we cannot but be agreed that the fixed and determinate sense of the words is the ultimate submission to Christ of every soul.

The only possible source of disagreement would seem to lie in the varying meaning we may give to the words Submission to Christ. Will it be an enforced submission, merely outward, and therefore incomplete? Or will it be willing, inward, and perfect?

The answer to the question will depend upon whether

we look at the matter from a physical or a spiritual standpoint. If from the former, we may think of these rebels as beaten in fight, deprived of weapons, fettered and imprisoned, and so restrained from all outward acts of rebellion, but still in heart full of bitter longing for fresh opportunity, and full of malignity and hatred. Now would that be really worth singing about? Would it content the Son of God? In nothing more than that could He see of the travail of His Soul and be satisfied? But who can help confessing, looking at the matter from a spiritual point of view, such victory to be no victory at all? In spiritual spheres coercion can never be conquest. A man beaten down in fight, crippled, disarmed, immured, gagged, and blinded, is restrained from such rebellion as ordinarily troubles an earthly government; but merely to deprive a man of the ability to sin outwardly against God, to sin, that is, with hand, or voice, or eye, is not at all to touch the sin for which Jesus lived and died. This is nothing less than sin of soul; it is ignorance of mind, enmity of heart, rebellion of will; and it seems to me the fixed and determinate sense of the words under review points to a victory which means the vanquishing of these.

If this reasoning is felt to be just, the position to which it leads us is something like this : We believe in the coming universal reign of Christ, and we believe that reign will be spiritual, that it will be dominion over mind and heart and will. What follows from that? Does it not appear to follow that the far-off divine event can only be brought about by the turning of every soul of man from sin to righteousness? Not to freedom from pain and sorrow. I cannot see that. To think of all men, in the ages to come, being made alike, in the possession of perfect peace and happiness, is not possible. We have been far too much in the habit of confounding things, and have commonly spoken of righteousness as though of necessity it meant happiness. Experience tells us it does not. And with every wish to avoid exaggeration, and declining to use unscriptural expressions, I cannot find, either in the Bible or in reason, any hope that sinful men will ever be relieved of some, to say no more, of the penalties of sin. But, notwithstanding this, it does seem to me possible that the universal reign of righteousness may be brought about in the way we have been considering.

It occurs to me that to nothing more than this confusing of things, this neglect of using words in the fixed and determinate sense that belongs to them, is owing the existence of the theory which speaks of sin as endless. Confounding righteousness with happiness, and not seeing how some men could ever be peaceful or joyful, people have jumped to the conclusion that some men can never be saved from sin. But we may probably come to see they can, if we remember that our Christian faith requires us to think of a righteousness which is not incompatible with exceeding sorrow and bitter pain; or if, in other words, we remember how the one righteous Man was also the Man of sorrows, and the most righteous thing ever done on this earth was also the most agonizing. And it was He, and not some fancied incarnate happiness, who said, I will draw all unto Myself.

It is, I think, the same tendency to mix things up that has led many good men to accept another view as to the means whereby the reign of righteousness is to be established. I speak now of the destruction of evil men, either by an act of annihilation, or by the soul dying of evil as the body dies of disease. To my mind this theory, satisfactory as it is said to be to many thoughtful people, is repugnant both to Scripture and to reason. It involves a disbelief in the omnipotence of God, for we cannot doubt His will. I know that many who have no sympathy with annihilation views will not agree with me in this. Dr. Beet, for example, in his recent book, speaks many times of the divine purpose of salvation as embracing the whole human race, but infers that in some cases that purpose will not be accomplished. Now it may be that I am dense, I do not think I am prejudiced, but to such faculties as I possess such an inference is incomprehensible. And in the interest of Wesley's phrase about employing words in their fixed and determinate sense, I really must be allowed to growl at Dr. Beet a little. If we will all think of it, we shall agree there can be no greater heresy than the allowing ourselves in religious matters the use of words in a sense that does not properly belong to them; this can be little less than the abomination of desolation standing in the holy place. But what is the natural and proper meaning of the word Omnipotent? Isaiah told us the *olam* God fainteth not neither is weary. Is that true only in the physical sphere? I should like to hear the Prophet and the Professor discuss the question, and some day I hope I may be permitted to do so. Meanwhile, to believe in the Lord God Omnipotent, and also to believe that such a poor thing as we know the human will to be is able to outmatch and defy omnipotence, is altogether out of my power. And whenever I read or think of the annihilation theory, a vision appears to me, far away in the future universe of man, of some kind of heaven, not very large, and not very thickly populated, and not very cheerful; while all the rest of that universe is one vast sepulchre, on which I can see no epitaph except, The Failure of the Almighty God.

Resuming, and completing, our inquiry, let us ask what the texts of Scripture, now to be quoted, will teach us if only we adhere to the rule about the use of words. Many such texts might be given, but I will only mention three. These have been selected because they are apparently both strong and clear, and because they are often overlooked in discussions on the subject engaging us. Professor Beet, for instance, in the book we have spoken of, does not allude to any of them.

The first is:—

John i. 29. Behold the Lamb of God, which taketh away the sin of the world.

The word translated Taketh-away may mean Lift, or Bear; but in any case the idea is that of separating sin from the world. It is not atoning for, and it is not removing the guilt or the punishment of sin; it is taking away the Sin of the world. And World is not our old acquaintance *aiōn;* it is the same World that we have in the words, The World was made by Him, and the World knew Him not. The Sin, considered as a whole, of that World, also considered as a whole, He taketh away. This seems to repeat what the Baptist had earlier said in a more figurative fashion, He will throughly, not partially, cleanse His floor; and He will gather His wheat into the garner, but the chaff He will burn up with unquenchable fire.

Our second text is :—

<blockquote>Rev. v. 13. And every created thing which is in the heaven, and on the earth, and under the earth, and on the sea, and all things that are in them, heard I saying, In Him that sitteth on the throne, and in the Lamb, the blessing, and the honour, and the glory, and the dominion, to the certainties of the certainties.</blockquote>

Dr. Beet tells us, speaking of some other passages, that the speaker in his use of words is limited by his mental horizon. I readily agree. But in the quotation before us the question rises, How could anybody's mental horizon be wider than this? Every created thing ascribes Dominion, which, to say nothing of the other qualities, must be a matter of experience; and it is spoken of as an *olam* of *olams*. I cannot see how words, if we take them in their fixed and determinate meaning, can possibly be clearer, stronger, or more comprehensive. And as for wishing to limit their scope, are we not all created things?

The last text is from St. Paul:—

<blockquote>1 Cor. xv. 28. And when all things have been subjected unto Him, then shall the Son also Himself be subjected to Him that did subject all things unto Him, that God may be all in all.</blockquote>

The full force of the Greek in the last words is, we are told, All things in all men; or, as we might say colloquially, Everything in everybody. And lest there should be any possibility of thinking that All means here something less than that, the context plainly tells us that the only exception to the All is Him who did subject all things. John Wesley's note on the passage is as follows :—

"All things (consequently all persons) without any interruption, without the intervention of any creature, without the opposition of any enemy, shall be subordinate to God. All shall say, 'My God, and my all.'"

And here I must take my leave. In so doing, let me say if I have written a word to grieve anyone it has been unintentional, and I am sorry. But this does not apply to the inventors of the Hebrew points. Especially if I have said anything against the truth do I pray to be forgiven, and ask to be set right; for I would fain be up to the standard of Socrates, and be willing to be refuted if it can be shown that I have said anything not true.

INDEX

A.

	PAGE
Acts iv. 21	212
,, x. 38	197
adh	36 ff.
ady	28 ff.
"Age-long," etc.	174
Aiōnios defined	175
Amen, meaning of	130
Amos i. 11	20
Annihilation theory	252
Aristotle on *aiōn*	140
Arnold, Matthew, quoted	13
Athanasian Creed	109, 240

B.

Bacon, Lord, quoted	201
Banks, Professor, quoted	124
Beet, Professor, quoted	242 f., 252
Blessing, Hebrew	131
Browning quoted	79, 117
Burial Service	151, 240
Burke, Edmund, on judgment	184
Burning up of chaff, etc.	223
Butler, Bishop, quoted	87

C.

Carlyle quoted	63
Certainties of the Certainties	128
Chief of Certainties	10, 104
1 Chronicles iv. 27	27
,, xxviii. 9	17, 19
,, xxix. 10–11	131
2 ,, ix. 2	68
,, xxxiii. 7	83
Clark, Adam, quoted	123
Coleridge, S. T., on weighing words	154
Colossians i. 26	156, 162, 172

	PAGE
Common Prayer, Book of	9
1 Corinthians ii. 6–8	167
,, iii. 18	167
,, iv. 17	178
,, v. 5	217
,, x. 11	164
,, xv. 28	254
,, xv. 28, Wesley on	255
2 ,, iv. 4	168
,, iv. 17	178
,, iv. 18	180
,, v. 1	180
Cursing, English	131
,, Hebrew	131

D.

Daniel iii. 27	38
,, xii. 2	96
Death, meaning of	195
De Foe quoted	137
De Quincey quoted	2
Deuteronomy iv. 24	221
,, iv. 45	36
,, xxx. 15	192
,, xxxi. 28	61
,, xxxii. 7	102
,, xxxii. 9–12	105
,, xxxii. 26–27	106
,, xxxiii. 27	115
"Divine Humanity, Gospel of," quoted	114, 210
Doxologies, the	129

E.

Ecclesiastes iii. 11	66, 79
,, iii. 14	73

INDEX. 257

	PAGE
Ecclesiastes xi. 3	75
,, xii. 5	88
Edwards, Jonathan, on Hell	238
eis translating *ad*	137
Ephesians ii. 2, 7	156
,, iii. 9	172
Ewing on *aidios* and *ad*	125
Exaggeration of stern texts	241 ff.
Exodus xx. 16	50
,, xxii. 12–13	51
,, xxii. 26	25
,, xxxii. 13	70
,, xxxiii. 5	30, 32
,, xxxiii. 22	24
,, xxxv. 20	42
,, xl. 15	71
Ezekiel vii. 19	213
,, vii. 20	29, 32
,, xvi. 7	31
,, xviii. 20	193
Ezra iii. 13	24

F.

Failure of Almighty God	253
Fire, meaning of	221, 224
Fixities in the N.T.	162 ff.
Fixity	76
Forgiveness, meaning of	219

G.

Galatians i. 4	168
,, i. 5	129, 132
Genesis ii. 17	192
,, iii. 22	90 ff.
,, vi. 3	94
,, vi. 4	82
,, xiii. 12	25
,, xvii. 1	6
,, xxxi. 24, 51–52	57
,, xlix. 27	16, 22
Gray's "Elegy" quoted	179

H.

Habakkuk iii. 6	16, 20
Hawthorne quoted	50
Hebrew Bible	3
Hebrews, Epistle to the	3
,, i. 2	162
,, i. 8	10, 27, 119

	PAGE
Hebrews v. 6	143
,, v. 9	183 f.
,, vi. 2	183 f.
,, vi. 5	166
,, vi. 6	220
,, vii. 16, 24, 25, 28;	144 ff.
,, ix. 12	183 f.
,, ix. 14	178
,, ix. 15	180 ff.
,, ix. 26	165
,, x. 12, 15	144
,, xii. 1	62
,, xiii. 8	152
,, xiii. 20	180 ff.
Hebrew Parallelism	81, 103
,, prophets	7
,, thought in Greek words,	14, 120, 136, 177
,, vowel points	3 ff., 7
His mercy endureth for ever?	74 f.
Hosea ii. 19	88

I.

Interpretation, rules of	7
Isaiah iv. 4	222
,, ix. 6	20
,, xiv. 13–14	34
,, xxvi. 4	113
,, xxxii. 14–15	70
,, xxxii. 17–19	89
,, xxxiv. 10	96 ff.
,, xxxv. 10	68
,, xl. 19–20	111
,, xl. 28	110
,, xlii. 14	69, 80
,, xlv. 17	88
,, xlvi. 4	112
,, xlvi. 9	104
,, xlvii. 7	95
,, li. 9	102–107
,, li. 10–11	107
,, liv. 8	101
,, lv. 4	54
,, lvii. 15	15, 21
,, lviii. 12	99
,, lxi. 4	69
,, lxi. 19	68

S

J.

	Page
James i. 27	205
Jehovah as Love	109
Jeremiah ii. 20	82
,, ii. 32	31
,, v. 22	77
,, xvii. 4	96
,, xx. 11	96
,, xxxi. 4	39
,, li. 39	96
Job vii. 16	90
,, x. 17	54
,, xiv. 14	24, 25
,, xv. 34	48
,, xvi. 7	16, 22
,, xvi. 18-19	58
,, xix. 23-24	19
,, xx. 4-5	26
,, xxviii. 20-21	68, 78
,, xxix. 11-12	55
,, xxx. 23	35
,, xl. 10	38
John i. 29	253
,, iii. 36	199 ff.
,, iv. 14	136
,, v. 24	190
,, vi. 53-54	199 ff.
,, vi. 58	149
,, viii. 35	152
,, viii. 51	150
,, ix. 32	159, 161
,, x. 28	150, 191
,, xii. 32	230, 243
,, xii. 32, Bishop Westcott on	243
,, xiii. 8	150
,, xiv. 9	197
,, xiv. 16	152
,, xvii. 3	189, 196
1 John ii. 17	147
,, iii. 14-17	206
,, iv. 18	211
,, v. 11-12	199 f.
,, v. 13	189
Jonah ii. 6	73
Joshua xxiv. 21-22	60
,, xxiv. 26-27	59
Jude 6	124
,, 13	149
,, 24-25	129, 132

	Page
Judges ii. 1	84
,, iii. 26	24
,, xiv. 8	47
,, xx. 38	34
,, xx. 48	26

K.

1 Kings viii. 5	43
,, xviii. 21	160
2 ,, v. 27	85
,, ix. 22	24 f.

L.

Leviticus iv. 13	68, 78
,, viii. 3	42
,, xxiv. 16	42
,, xxv. 32	79
Liddell and Scott on *aiōn*	138
Life, meaning of	194 ff.
,, Tree of	91 ff.
lolam	82 ff.
Love defeats Terror	247
,, defined	198
Luke i. 33	146
,, i. 70	159, 161
,, ii. 29-32	185
,, xii. 15	194
,, xv. 32	193, 242
,, xvi. 8	167
,, xvi. 9	180 ff.
,, xviii. 29-30	166, 187
,, xx. 35	166

M.

MacDonald, Dr. George, quoted	186
Malachi iii. 3	222
,, iii. 5	53
Mark iii. 29	150, 218 ff.
,, ix. 47	224 ff.
,, x. 17	191, 204
,, xi. 14	149
Matthew iii. 10-12	222
,, vii. 11	198
,, xii. 32	166
,, xiii. 39	154, 163, 223
,, xxiv. 3	164
,, xxv. 46	123, 188, 205, 210 ff.

INDEX.

	PAGE
Matthew xxv. 46, Wesley's note on	215
Maurice, F. D., quoted	119
Melchisedec, Mr. Stead on	143
Micah i. 2	53
moad	32, 40, 41
molam	80 ff.
Mystery, meaning in N.T.	172

N.

Napoleon quoted	75
Numbers i. 2	43 f.
,, viii. 4	26
,, ix. 2–3	33, 34
,, xiii. xiv.	45 f.
,, xvi.	46 f.
,, xx. 2	43 f.
,, xxxii. 13	24
,, xxxv. 12	42, 44

O.

O King, live for ever!	67, 90
olam mercy	113
,, landmark	69, 99
,, love	101

P.

1 Peter i. 25	142
,, v. 10	178
2 Peter i. 11	180 ff.
,, ii. 9	212
Philemon 15	174
Plato on *aiōn*	139
Plumptre, Dr. E. H., on *olam*	64
Pope, Alex., quoted	116, 229 f.
Preconception	121, 187
Proverbs xxii. 28	69
,, xxv. 20	37
Psalms i. 5	48
,, xxi. 6	19
,, xxiv. 7–8	115
,, xxxi. 1	83
,, xxxii. 9	29, 31
,, xlv. 6	10, 27
,, xlix. 11	77
,, lxxiv. 8	41
,, lxxv. 2	41

	PAGE
Psalms lxxvii. 5	81, 102
,, lxxvii. 19–20	106
,, lxxxii. 1	48
,, lxxxix. 35–37	72 f.
,, xc. 8	66, 78
,, ciii. 5	29, 32
,, civ. 19	33
,, cvi. 30	79
,, cxix. 52	80
,, cxxxiii. 3	193
,, cxxxix. 23–24	94
,, cxliii. 3	69, 80
,, cxlv. 13	146

R.

Revelation, import of the word	7
Revelation i. 18	127
,, iii. 15	62
,, iv. 10	133
,, v. 13	254
,, vii. 11–12	129, 133
,, xiv. 6	180 ff.
,, xix. 3	9, 133
,, xx. 10	134
,, xxii. 5	133
Revised Version, the	12
Romans i. 20	124
,, xii. 2	167
,, xvi. 25	171
,, xvi. 26	177
Ruth iv. 9–11	52

S.

Salt, use of	226
Salted with fire	225 f.
1 Samuel iii. 14	85
,, xii. 3	55
,, xii. 5	56
2 Samuel i. 24	30
,, xii. 10	84
Sd, sdh, etc.	5 ff.
Septuagint, the	3
Socrates quoted	255
Sonnet on the *olam* God	111
Swift quoted	40

T.

Tennyson quoted	117, 208
Terror defeated by love	247

	PAGE
2 Thess. i. 7–9	123, 216 ff.
,, ii. 16	. 183 f.
1 Timothy i. 17	. 146
,, v. 6	. 193
,, vi. 16	. 178
,, vi. 17–19	168, 206
2 ,, i. 10	. 172
,, iv. 9	. 154
Titus i. 2	171 f.
,, ii. 12	. 168
Tormented, or Tossed?	. 134

U

Unquenchable explained . 226
Unto the ages of the ages 13, 121

V

	PAGE
Vowel points, Hebrew	3 ff, 7

W

Wesley, John .	. 208
,, on Hell	. 239
,, note on 1 Cor. xv. 28	255
,, ,, Matt. xxv. 46	215
Wesleyan hymns quoted	209, 245
Westcott, Bishop, on *aiōnios*	141
,, ,, note on John xii. 32	. 243
Whately's "English Synonyms" quoted	. 122
Wordsworth quoted .	108, 207

www.ingramcontent.com/pod-product-compliance
Lightning Source LLC
Chambersburg PA
CBHW032134230426
43672CB00011B/2332